MODERN MANHOOD

Conversations About the Complicated World of Being a Good Man Today

MODERN MANHOOD

CLEO STILLER

Tiller Press
New York London Toronto Sydney New Delhi

TILLER PRESS

An Imprint of Simon & Schuster, Inc.
1230 Avenue of the Americas
New York, NY 10020

This publication contains the opinions and ideas of its author.
The names and identifying characteristics of some individuals have been
changed. This publication is intended to provide helpful and informative
material on the subjects addressed in the publication. It is sold with the
understanding that the author and publisher are not engaged in
rendering medical, health, or any other kind of personal professional
services in the book. The reader should consult his or her medical,
health, or other competent professional before adopting any of the
suggestions in this book or drawing inferences from it.

The author and publisher specifically disclaim all
responsibility for any liability, loss, or risk, personal or otherwise,
which is incurred as a consequence, directly or indirectly,
of the use and application of any of the contents of this book.

First Tiller Press hardcover edition November 2019

TILLER PRESS and colophon are trademarks of Simon & Schuster, Inc.

For information about special discounts for bulk purchases,
please contact Simon & Schuster Special Sales at 1-866-506-1949
or business@simonandschuster.com.

The Simon & Schuster Speakers Bureau can bring authors
to your live event. For more information, or to book an event,
contact the Simon & Schuster Speakers Bureau at 1-866-248-3049
or visit our website at www.simonspeakers.com.

Interior design by Lewelin Polanco

Manufactured in the United States of America

1 3 5 7 9 10 8 6 4 2

Library of Congress Cataloging-in-Publication Data is available.

ISBN 978-1-9821-3201-9
ISBN 978-1-9821-3205-7 (ebook)

For those trying to leave the world
a better place than they found it.

Contents

MODERN MANHOOD

Introduction

Here are three self-evident truths: the Harvey Weinsteins of the world need to go, sexual assault is wrong, and women and men should be on equal footing. If you disagree with any of the aforementioned, then this book isn't for you.

But if you're still here, you're probably one of the good guys—and you're probably feeling frustrated and exasperated, or simply thinking *WTF?*, when it comes to the current national conversation surrounding #MeToo, masculinity, and the relationship between women and men. You might have even rolled your eyes at a group text with your friends or while you were scrolling through Facebook or Twitter and said, "This has all just gone a little too far." (Not that you'd openly cop to that IRL, for fear of getting chewed out.)

If so, then this book is for you—because you get it, but you've also likely found yourself in countless experiences or conversations recently where the situation feels gray, at best. For example, who hasn't had a date like Aziz Ansari? Or, as a manager, how are you supposed to mentor your female employees in this climate? Or, if this is a post–#MeToo world, how come men are often still shamed for making less than their female partners? Can you still watch Louis C.K.?!

How come you're always being made to feel like crap if you ask these questions out loud? And when do we start talking about solutions instead of just putting people down?

Welcome to *Modern Manhood*.

This book is a manual and a resource that I hope will shed some light on all the gray areas out there, focusing on conversations you are already having with your friends, your dates, your family, and yourself. Each chapter will cover a different area of your personal life, from money and sex to dating and work. I've talked to experts, celebrities and influencers, and folks just like yourself to see what other people are thinking and doing about these exact questions.

So, you can think of this book as a crowdsourced document of sorts. It's not prescriptive and it has no rules. You can take what you like and leave what you don't.

Oh, and then there's me: Cleo Stiller, a journalist, television host, and regular shmegular human who is going to help synthesize all of this information. Also, I'm a lady. Hi.

I started writing this book because I was getting a lot of DMs from men in the aftermath of #MeToo. These were men, mostly straight, who wanted to be thought of as decent dudes, and *they* certainly thought of themselves that way, but it seemed to them like everything they were taught about how to be a "good guy" is now being called into question. And, to make matters worse, there are a lot of mixed messages out there. The seemingly harmless workplace banter at happy hour that's no longer harmless, the conflicting messages you're getting about consent during a hookup while still trying to be an assertive guy, and why, if we're striving toward equality, are you still on the hook for paying for dates? Does this sound at all familiar?

This is the kind of stuff that you haven't typically had to think much about—and maybe you still don't—but times are changing. Some men are avoiding one-on-one meetings with women in the office entirely because #MeToo has them so spooked. Yes, things have gotten confusing!

And yet, if you ask many therapists, relationship coaches, and activists who work in this space, they actually see this time as a positive. This is an opportunity to be more thoughtful about things we've previously taken for granted and maybe could use an upgrade.

"What we're talking about here is changing social norms about what is acceptable," Jackson Katz said in a recent episode of National Public Radio's *TED Radio Hour*[1] Ted Talk about the impact of #MeToo. Katz is a world-renowned speaker on promoting gender equality and a cofounder of the Mentors in Violence Prevention program, one of the longest-running gender violence prevention programs in North America.

"I think that's really the ultimate issue because so many of the problems that are surfacing are not just about individual perpetrators who are horrible men. . . . While I think it was important that as high-profile men, [Harvey Weinstein's and Bill Cosby's] cases became cultural touchstones, it also distorted the issue a little bit because their behavior is so awful. . . . A lot of men could distance themselves from them and say, 'This guy is just sick. That's not me,'" he says. "I think that real reckoning is not with the pathological individuals, but it's with the norms that have guided so many of us for so long."

But what do *you* think of #MeToo and its potential impact? The men I spoke to really ran the gamut—some staunchly in favor and others … well, they're a little unclear about where it's all going.

> "I feel as though #MeToo created a more consensual culture. You can be super old school and bemoan it. But in this new world, people get to speak up and ask for what they really want." —*Colin Adamo,* Hooking Up and Staying Hooked *founder*

> "I guess my concern is: What is the goal? What is a reasonable and fair ask of us as men (humans), and at what point do we go beyond what is healing for society?" —*Rich, 32*

"I have mixed feelings about #MeToo in general. On one hand, I think it's a great concept and that it's well past time for us to call out the horrible behavior and abuses of power by people. . . . But I worry that as it grows it becomes a McCarthy-like situation where a mere allegation is enough to ruin someone, and evidence doesn't matter. . . . " —*Stephan Badyna, 34,* A Pod Amongst Men *host*

This book is an attempt to bring many different, thoughtful, and proactive voices together in one spot—not to ask them about meta-concepts, but to get granular, practical advice about real and practical situations you're finding yourself in.

For that reason, I structured this book exactly like your life goes down. From my vantage point, most of the questions I received can be grouped into these eight core areas: dating, sex, work, money, parenting, friends, self-care, and media. Within each area, I also wanted to drill down on a really specific question or situation that I've been asked about repeatedly. These scenarios may seem a little basic, but I specifically chose them for two reasons: 1) many people asked me about them, and 2) they're questions that are particularly vexing given the current cultural climate *right now*.

In addition, there are several basic archetypes of a man that I'll interrogate in the book: the pursuer, the aggressor, the leader, the provider, the protector, and the lone wolf. Some of these archetypes may seem outdated, others feel noble—but where do they fit into your life given everything happening *right now*?

This is not a heavily academic book. I know from my work that there are many very intelligent people thinking critically about what it means to be a "good guy" today. Often, their names don't come with degrees after them. They're not all academics or clinicians. These folks have been thinking about what modern masculinity looks like and you can find their wisdom in various places from YouTube videos to Twitter threads to blog posts, but this book seeks to give a sort of inside track, like if you could grab a beer with them here's what they'd tell you. They certainly don't represent one singular "male experience," either, hailing from all parts of the country with different ethnic backgrounds, political affiliations, and income levels. Of the people who shared their stories and opinions with me, some were comfortable using their full names and others, understandably, preferred to have their identities obscured. In those cases, their names have been changed and I use only a first name. Those who spoke to me in a professional capacity used their proper names and titles, of course.

By now (or perhaps for the past few pages) you've probably been asking yourself: Wait, but why is a woman writing this?

That is a fair question! What are my qualifications for talking to men about being a man?

First of all, the majority of this book will be the offerings from men (with some female and nonbinary perspectives woven in). I'm just your guide. The way I see it, we live in a particularly fractured society, and it's my goal as a reporter to tell stories that help us realize we're all on the same team.

Take a look at the current landscape when it comes to #MeToo: there are a lot of articles and books and videos made about #MeToo by women for women. On the other side, there also some being made by men for men.

However, I didn't see a lot of content that was made for men by women.

I've sat in conversations with women and nonbinary folks and thought, "Everyone needs to hear this." And I've sat in conversations with self-identified men, thinking, "Everyone needs to hear *this*." I think it's vital to have a spread of different perspectives at the table.

This is a reporting style that's defined my entire career.

Prior to writing this book, I created and hosted a television show for the cable network Fusion called *Sex.Right.Now. with Cleo Stiller*, where I conducted hundreds of interviews across the country with people across the gender spectrum about the ways that technology, politics, and pop culture are impacting the most intimate aspects of our personal lives. Topics on my show included everything from how smartphones are impacting our romantic relationships, the future of male birth control, and the rise of nonmonogamy. You may have heard of the Peabody Awards. Yeah, we were nominated for one of those.

Before my show, I got my start in journalism as a producer covering financial and business stories for Bloomberg. So, I like to say that my expertise is in talking about subjects that make people generally very uncomfortable: money and sex—and everything in between.

Over the course of my career, I've won a Gracie Award, been nominated for an Emmy Award (among many others), and have presented at multiple conferences and industry events about health and gender representation in the media. However, my real passion is asking deeply, deeply personal questions of people I don't know very well. I've gotten pretty good at getting personal without getting awkward, and I have a strict "no judgment" and "no stigma" approach.

That said, I want to be very clear about the fact that I'm not an expert. I don't have an advanced degree in sociology and psychology. I'm not a relationship counselor. I'm just a reporter with an extensive network and understanding of how certain cultural, political, and technological shifts have gotten us to where we are now.

And as an empathetic human, I want to see us move forward the best way possible.

Currently, we are at a collective cultural tipping point. That's not to say any of these issues are new—they are certainly not. But a hodgepodge of various factors (social, political, technological, generational) have gotten us to a place where it's not just academics or career lawmakers or lifelong community activists who are thinking about the ways women and men interact. Nowadays, even Joe Schmoe is wondering whether or not it's still cool to compliment a coworker on her outfit. Or whether his friend should be showing people that naked selfie from his hookup the other night.

I wrote this book because I don't want us to miss this opportunity to make a better system for women, men, and everyone in between—to interrogate aspects of our behavior that we've always taken for granted.

So, here we go.

Chapter 1
DATING

They met at a United Nations climate change summit. Rajiv, freshly thirty, had been living like a vagabond, traveling domestically and internationally for work over the last couple of years. He was personally looking to settle down and start a solid relationship with someone. The woman, Sarah, was British but her mother happened to be from the same Indian village as Rajiv's father. Sarah lived in London and was about to move to New Zealand—she also had a nomadic lifestyle. Rajiv took all of these similarities to heart and thought, "Wow, there is real potential here."

But Sarah wasn't so sure. She was sexually inexperienced and just looking for friendship. She said this to him multiple times over the course of the next several months. Rajiv tells me he wrote off her hesitation as inexperience. She asked for friendship; he kept making the moves. He made grand gestures, including a flight to New Zealand and, after enough persuading, moving her from New Zealand to the United States. Surprising no

one except him—it didn't last. Shortly after coming to the States, she left him to travel in Central
America. He was heartbroken, wondering what he
did wrong, when everyone else in his life was like,
"Dude, read the signs."

When he found out I was writing this book,
and particularly a part on dating, men and women,
and #MeToo, Rajiv immediately got in touch. He
wanted to explain himself to me and to do so he
used a scene from the Disney movie *Cinderella*.

Basically, it's that scene at the end of the ball
when the prince and Cinderella share a kiss. Then
the clock strikes and she jumps up to leave. He
tries to get her to stay, but she's like, "NO! I really
gotta go."

We all in the audience know she's about to turn
into a hot mess, so she really, really needs to jet.
But he grabs her wrist and tries to keep her there.
Then she runs away and he sends henchmen chas-
ing after her to get her back.

"I took away the belief that if I persisted
enough, she would realize my love was real," Rajiv
says. "What does this teach boys about how far to
push, reading nonverbal cues, or whether to accept
'Good-bye!' as enough to stop persisting?"

IS EVERYTHING YOU WERE
TAUGHT TO DO NOW CONSIDERED CREEPY?

Dating is awkward. It always has been.

Now take the natural confusion and fear of rejection and toss
in the worry that you'll do something to upset someone and be the
next #MeToo headline in your friend group. Woof. Intimidating.

Here's a sample from men I talked to about what it's like to
date today:

"I think #MeToo has caused a tremendous amount of uncertainty within men, like what are the boundaries?" —*Lucas Krump, 39*, Evryman *co-founder*

"I think right now dating is really weird because guys like me . . . I feel like sometimes we don't know what to do. . . . Is it okay to compliment somebody physically? Is it OK to compliment what they're wearing? Am I going to get slack for that? So I think that's been the biggest challenge, just knowing what to say. What is offensive now?" —*Brad Pankey, 31*, Modern Masculinity Project *podcast host*

"I think there was a certain terror at first, of just wondering if I'd done anything that somebody would think was inappropriate. Looking back, I thought I was fine—I didn't think there was anything that I'd done that was terrible. But I also recognized that any time that I'd done something that I was questioning whether it was appropriate, was when it involved me drinking alcohol. So I haven't drank alcohol since the #MeToo movement started." —*Adam, 33*

"I haven't been single during this entire movement. But it seems to me that I got out of the game just in time. I'd be terrified constantly." —*Austin, 36*

Men are spooked! And listen, I hear you.

Here's the thing, though. Precisely because dating is so fraught and personal, it makes for a great lens to look at some of the broader topics that will repeatedly come up in this book. Much of our society is built on old ideas and norms we haven't really reconsidered—things like gender roles, masculinity and femininity, nature versus nurture, and cultural sensitivity. We should have already been doing this, but the intense cultural divide around #MeToo is a loud whistle blow.

Let's start at the beginning. The issue underlying Rajiv's story hits at a classic male archetype: men as the pursuer.

"Persistence pays off," says Dominick Quartuccio. Quartuccio used to run a sales team with a $4 billion sales goal in midtown Manhattan, but left the corporate life to be an executive coach. He's now an international speaker, author of the book *Design Your Future*, and cohost of the podcast *Man Amongst Men*. To give you an idea of the kind of circles he runs in, he recently presented a workshop about masculinity at the renowned financial firm Goldman Sachs in New York City. He's learned a lot about men from his clients, who are, he tells me, "high-performing men who are publicly confident but privately confused." The type who think, "'Hey, I have everything that I ever worked for. . . . I have everything on paper. Everyone from the outside thinks my life is great, but on the inside I'm feeling restless and stressful.'"

Quartuccio is big into this notion of persistence sculpting how men think of themselves. It's a concept known as "the hero's journey."

"As guys, we look at these heroes who against all odds prevail, right?" he says. "However, many times the hero has been told no. Not necessarily in a social or sexual context, but in life, in business, in war, on the sporting fields. If he falls down, he gets back up and keeps going until he gets the prize. He's a relic."

What's one of the most iconic, deeply ingrained prizes at the end of the hero's journey? Boy wins the prize and gets the girl.

But where did the idea for this archetype come from?

You have to remember that marrying for love is a relatively new concept. For most of human history, marriage has been seen as a strategic way to broker alliances. In that context, women are seen as the property of the men in their family, to be traded for wealth and power. Dating, in the sense we think of it, didn't really start in the United States until around 1890. It was a result of the industrial revolution, when women and men left their villages to move to cities for work.

According to Moira Weigel, author of *Labor of Love: The Invention of Dating*,[1] the phrase "date" first made its way into print in 1896 in a weekly column for a Chicago newspaper by a writer named George Ade. The column, called "Stories of the Streets and Town," promised to give the paper's middle-class readership a look into the life of the working class. In this particular column, a young clerk at the paper suspected his girlfriend was seeing other people and asked her, "I s'pose the other boy's fillin' all my dates?"

Dating was something reserved for the working class. The middle-class version was known as "calling." Middle-class women didn't need to work, so suitors would "call" on the women at their home. "The ritual," says Weigel, "made men into agents in pursuit. It made women the objects of desire."

This is something that has stuck with us ever since—the idea that men are the pursuers and women are to be pursued. It's one of the classic archetypes of what makes "a man." From the men I talked to, I can say that some of you think this is bullshit, but you still play into it. Some of you never related to this and still don't. And some of you are straight old-school and definitely still subscribe to this idea.

"Pursuing, to me, is a hard job. You can be shot down very rapidly," Helen Fisher, Ph.D., says. "All my studies clearly indicate that men would be very, very happy if women invited them for the first date, or initiated the first kiss, or if women were the ones to call the following morning, or the ones to initiate sex. But women don't do it. I think that says a great deal about the fact that, in courtship, things don't change."

Dr. Fisher is a renowned biological anthropologist who specializes in the study of the evolution and future of human sex, love, marriage, gender differences in the brain, and, as she describes it, how your personality style shapes who you are and who you love.

She's the author of six books on the topic and the chief scientific advisor at Match.com. Basically, if you have a question about sex, gender, or brains and need a historical perspective, you call her up. I have several times over my career, actually.

"Men say that they would be happy if women initiated the first kiss, but women don't do it," Dr. Fisher says. "It's very interesting: women still want to be pursued, and I think they're going to continue to want to be pursued."

In a post-#MeToo world that's moving beyond the gender binary, I caution against making any blanket statements like Dr. Fisher tends to, but her point is well taken. The point here is there are a lot of mixed signals circulating in our culture right now. On the one hand, if you have a penis you're supposed to pursue in every realm of your life, professionally and personally. That's a lot of work! And, as I heard from a lot of guys, lately it's become confusing—and even a little scary. Because on the other hand, if you pursue in the wrong way you might offend someone or get in trouble.

"I think that we're moving into a very exciting time, where women are more and more allowed to take the initiative, and still a lot of them aren't taking that initiative," Dr. Fisher says. "But it's only because we are in this time of tremendous transition. As time goes by, particularly with [millennials], they are leading the way toward women being more assertive in courtship—and when everybody realizes that men do want women to be assertive in courtship, that that's appealing to them, more women will do it."

No wonder men are confused. The traditional roles of courtship and pursuit are blurring, and all the rules you were taught for how to chase a woman have been repealed. Instead, those tactics could now be considered creepy.

"Imagine a guy who was deathly afraid of approaching women before," Thomas Edwards, a dating coach based in California and founder of the company The Professional Wingman, says. "Oh my God, he might commit to celibacy now."

Dang!

Persistence used to make you the hero. Not anymore. And the

truth is, it's been on the outs for a while—in fact, a lot of you might have thought we had already left it in the past.

Think back to Rajiv's story. He was following the script he'd downloaded from one of our greatest romance stories: *Cinderella*. Much has been written about the bill of goods sold to women by Disney, but the truth is, we've taught men a fairy tale, too—the fairy tale of noble pursuit. Now I know a lot of you, including Dr. Fisher, are going to say, "Okay, but Rajiv aside, dogged pursuit mostly still works!" I hear you. I know countless couples who talk glowingly about how the man in the partnership "wore her down." Then they giggle and nuzzle noses. This is real. Persistence often works. However, it's also increasingly becoming viewed as creepy. What are we supposed to do with that?

Before we attempt to answer that question, I want to explore another question: Is the notion of male pursuit innate—is that behavior hardwired? Let's dig into what drives human behavior when it comes to gender.

I brought this question to Lise Eliot, Ph.D., a neuroscientist and professor at the Chicago Medical School of Rosalind Franklin University of Medicine and Science and the author of *Pink Brain, Blue Brain: How Small Differences Grow into Troublesome Gaps*. Dr. Eliot's research is centered on brain and gender development and she specializes in analyzing the interplay between innate biology, sociocultural factors, and individual experience in molding our brains and behavior.

In my first question to Dr. Eliot, I asked if this gendered behavior originates in the brain or from somewhere else. Dr. Eliot stopped me right there.

"Everything is in the brain," she says. "All of our behavior is coming from the brain, but the question is, how does that behavior get there? Are you born with it, or is it learned?"

I want to make sure to pause long enough on this idea so that it seeps in. All of our actions and thoughts come from the brain. But the question is: How does that behavior get there? How much of that is inbuilt before you're born? And how much did you learn along the way?

"We do think there's something, probably prenatal testosterone, that what I call 'biases' brain development in one direction or another, just like a tiny little tilt," she says. But Dr. Eliot says most researchers will tell you that the difference is negligible.

Look at something like risk-taking, Dr. Eliot says. Research shows that there's no question males take greater physical, financial, and sexual risks. But, she underscores, there's no gene for risk taking. While some will point to the role of hormones like testosterone, Dr. Eliot says that isn't really it, either. Rather, she says, it's cultural influence that encourages this behavior from an early age. For example, we encourage boys at an early age to be highly competitive with each other—but much less so for girls. When you win a competition, the brain releases testosterone, promoting a sense of status and decreasing your sense of doubt, says Dr. Eliot. In this way, from an early age we train young people with penises to be more comfortable with risk as a brain activity.

So, this notion of "hardwiring" that I heard referenced in a bunch of my interviews? "It's just so counterintuitive to how our brains actually develop," she says. "Anyone who has ever studied the brain knows that the brain is exquisitely plastic." Moreover, we all come equipped with the same chemicals. Men and women are born with both testosterone and estrogen. It's just a matter of proportions that differentiates them.

The idea of the "masculine" and "feminine" energies also came up in a lot of my interviews, so much so that I had to dig into it. Humans have a long, long history of ascribing "masculine" and "feminine" qualities to nongendered things (like chemicals). Take, for instance, the yin and yang of Taoism, or Shakti and Shiva in some Eastern religions. Shakti is known as the feminine energy. She represents the great mother who nourishes all life. Her counterpart, Shiva, is masculine energy. He represents consciousness. Shiva is the vessel that Shakti fills with water and life.

Historically, these notions didn't describe people with penises versus people with vaginas. It was understood that each person was born with their own individual proportion of the two complementing energies. In other words, each human has masculine and feminine energy within them. I bring this up in the first chapter of the book because we're going to talk a lot about "what men do," and it's important to put these gender scripts in historical and cultural context. In many cases, and for many centuries, not everyone reduced human behavior to the binaries we take for granted now. To examine our current view of them, let's look at some macro trends of modern culture.

The first is that men are frequently put into a box. There's a whole national conversation around this idea called "Man Box culture." Basically, the idea is that we're taught "that men are in charge, which means [that] women are not," Tony Porter says in his Ted Talk.

Tony Porter is the CEO of the organization A Call to Men, which provides education all over the world for healthy, respectful manhood. Porter is legit. He's an advisor to the National Football League, National Basketball Association, National Hockey League, Major League Soccer, and Major League Baseball. Basically, he is working with all of our country's top athletes to reshape masculinity.

In his Ted Talk,[2] he continues explaining what we teach men. "That men lead and [women] should just follow and do what we say. That men are superior [and] women are inferior. That men are strong and women are weak. That women are of less value and the property of men, and objects, particularly sexual objects," he says.

Porter's Ted Talk has racked up more than 3 million views. In it, Porter lays out what he calls the Man Box. (He got the term from Paul Kivel, who wrote the book *Men's Work: How to Stop the Violence That Tears Our Lives Apart*.[3] Kivel helped develop the term "Act Like a Man Box" with the Oakland Men's Project in the early 1980s.)

Here's a visualization. It's a series of qualities men are instructed to embody:

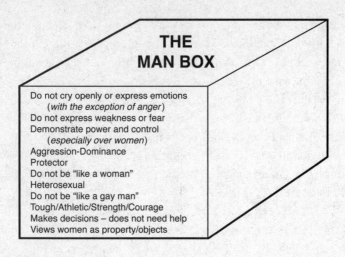

THE
MAN BOX

Do not cry openly or express emotions
     (*with the exception of anger*)
Do not express weakness or fear
Demonstrate power and control
     (*especially over women*)
Aggression-Dominance
Protector
Do not be "like a woman"
Heterosexual
Do not be "like a gay man"
Tough/Athletic/Strength/Courage
Makes decisions – does not need help
Views women as property/objects

This idea of the Man Box has gotten so much play in men's circles that, okay, well, you know Axe body spray? The parent company, Unilever, commissioned a study called "The Man Box: A Study on Being a Young Man in the U.S., UK, and Mexico."

What did it find?

"Young men reap certain benefits from staying inside the Man Box: it provides them with a sense of belonging, of living up to what is expected of them," it reads. "Friends and parents may praise them. However, when those same norms tell men to be aggressive all the time, to repress emotions, and to fight every time someone threatens them, the Man Box demands that they pretend to be someone they are not, and study results show how violent and lonely the resulting life can be."[4]

Someone else who has an interesting perspective on masculinity is Alex Schmider. Alex is the associate director of trans representation at the LGBTQ advocacy group GLAAD. He's made quite a name for himself within his industry, working behind the scenes with TV networks and film studios on their inclusive representation of transgender communities in the media. So much so that in 2017 he made *Forbes*'s enviable 30 Under 30 list in the media category.

As a trans man, Schmider has had the opportunity to think

critically about what masculinity means to him and what aspects of it he will and won't participate in, more so than say the average cis man. Here's what he came up with: "This affects every member of society . . . cisgender boys and men are not given nearly enough space or encouragement to be vulnerable and open with themselves, to familiarize with their emotions, to communicate their boundaries and needs, to respond to the boundaries and needs of others, and to develop meaningful relationships using all of the above interpersonal skills. External messages of inadequacy based on unchallenged conventions of gender can internalize and become a perpetual cycle of self-criticism and 'not enoughness'—punishing them and the people around them."

How does this relate to dating? Basically, men are still trying to fit into a very specific definition of what it means to "be a man" even if it doesn't feel completely authentic to them, and it reflects in how they date. I can give you an example. Meet Clint.

As #MeToo was unfolding, he sat down and reconsidered his "own thoughts, behavior, and conditioning," he told me. He changed "pretty drastically," he said, adding that it felt like being in a fun house of distorted mirrors, then walking outside and seeing things as they really are. One of his areas of change was how he approaches dating, specifically valuing emotional connection over physical attraction.

"I feel more whole, and thus more valuable to a potential partner, and less willing to indulge in the old, destructive paradigm play of 'man chases woman, she lets herself be caught,' et cetera," he says. "I'm worth the chase, too, and really, it shouldn't be a chase. Connection, if true, is easy, fun, honest, and fair." You're worth the chase, too. Like Clint, you may need to mature beyond a narrow view of masculinity to reexamine how you want to date.

Besides shifting cultural norms, the other component complicating dating that we can't overlook is the changing way of how people meet people.

Hint: they're doing it on the internet.

In many ways, the impact of technology is great and gives us tons of access to an unprecedented number of people. But it's also impersonal and allows us to fail on a massive scale. There are a slew of factors specific to the way we're dating that didn't exist ten years ago, meaning it's not only your parents who can't relate, but even a guy who was off the market in 2000 can't relate. (For reference, Match.com first launched in 1995, but if you were online dating back in 1995, let's just say you were a *real* early adopter.)

One in five people met their current partner using a dating app. Forty percent of Americans online date, according to a recent eHarmony survey.[5] Furthermore, a 2018 survey by the dating site Badoo[6] revealed that adults are spending 10 hours a week on dating apps, breaking down to roughly 85 minutes a day for men and 79 minutes a day for women. We don't need dating experts to tell us that online dating has irrevocably changed the game, but I found some anyway.

"The way we communicate through technology is very different from the way we communicate in person," Laurie Davis, the founder of eFlirt, a service that helps people build online dating profiles, says. Davis also founded The Worthy One, which focuses on coaching professionally successful but romantically frustrated women—and she's the author of *Love at First Click: The Ultimate Guide to Online Dating*.

Some people are more confident and clever online. Many are more forward—and not in a good way, says Davis. Fifty-three percent of women between the ages of eighteen and thirty-four have received a dick pic, according to a 2017 survey by YouGov.[7] That's a lot of dicks.

I'd go out on a limb and guess most of them were not asked for, either.

Given the differences of communicating in short text bursts and pixels, it's even more beneficial to think through what you're saying. Obviously, don't send unsolicited dick pics. But also consider what you're conveying, since it won't have the context data of facial expressions and vocal intonations, says Davis. Another opportunity online dating gives us to think through is what we actually want in a partner. In your pocket, with a few taps on your phone, you have access to thousands of people. Who do you want to date? The spread of choices can be overwhelming.

Thomas Edwards, the Professional Wingman, told me a story of a female client he once had. They went to an event in Washington, D.C., and he pretended to go to the bathroom so he could watch her in action. She positioned herself near men, with her body open, and smiled. All of the men near her had their heads bowed. When Edwards walked by and checked, they were on their phones, swiping. With an attractive woman, looking to date, standing right in front of them!

"Social media has given us so much exposure to what the fantasy of what our lives could look like, and we cling so much to that fantasy that we don't want to live in the reality," Edwards says. "It's a lot easier to live in what *could be* than what *is*."

Oh, by the way, Davis and Edwards are married. How cute, right? They met online.

One thing I'll point out is that online dating takes one question out of the mix. Everyone is there explicitly to meet other people. How many times have you heard someone say not to hit on women at the gym, since they're not there to date? At least online, you know there's some generalized interest.

#MeToo has made men more cautious and more aware of the ways that they interact, and it's affecting how men approach (or rather, in some cases, don't approach) potential dates.

"I hear them really questioning so much and being more hesitant to approach women," Davis says. "There was always a bit of anxiety there, but now there's even more of a hesitancy."

What's the solution?

"Men can't walk through life being afraid of what's going to happen, or are they going to do something inappropriate," Laurie Davis says. "If they are clear on their values and they're strong in that, they have to trust themselves. But I think a lot of this hesitation and anxiety comes across because they don't trust themselves."

When I pushed back on this idea, because it seems to me that a lot of men trust themselves perhaps a bit too much and it has only gotten them in deserved trouble, Davis brought up another component.

"I think listening is a big part of it," she says. "Trusting that you're not going to harm someone and you're going to really be in support of building a relationship means listening to the other person. Maybe it's both, maybe it's trust and listening."

Mmhmm. You can't see me, but I'm nodding my head.

One last thought from Davis: "It's also okay for men to ask for clarification on something, if they're not clear on what's being said."

This one is major. We don't encourage men or women to ask, check in, or verbalize when it comes to pretty much anything of an intimate nature, as you'll see in the Sex chapter, the Money chapter, the Self, Health, and Porn chapter … yeah, all of it. But one major way you can avoid coming off as a creep when you don't mean to? "Hey, I know it might be kinda awkward to ask you this, but with everything happening right now, I'd just like to make sure you're comfortable with me doing XYZ." See? It's not so hard.

On a similar note, openly talking about casual hookups carries much less of a social stigma than it has before. One side effect is that you may think everyone is boning all the time. And if you're not boning as much as you think you should be, you may be pursuing women very aggressively. Millennials have acquired a reputation for being the "Hookup Generation"—meaning that everyone thinks folks in their twenties and thirties are having more random, noncommitted sexual interactions than previous generations. There are two quick things to point out here, though. 1) With dating apps, and just the general ease of communication, we definitely have access to more people than ever before. But that doesn't necessarily mean we're having more sex. 2) Millennials are marrying later than ever. So, yes, there's probably more nonmarital sex going on than before.

"I want to tell you a couple things," Jaclyn Friedman, author of *Unscrewed: Women, Sex, Power and How to Stop Letting the System Screw Us All*, says. "First of all, the hookup culture is horseshit and doesn't exist."

Certain studies[8] point to the fact that millennials are actually having *less* sex than prior generations. Of course, studies in this area are often unreliable. It's extremely difficult to track how often people have sex, so we rely on self-reporting. This may come as a shock to you, but sometimes people lie about their sex lives. A real caution about the implications of the "hook up culture" reputation, according to Friedman, is that this reputation gives us the impression that everyone we know is having tons more sex than we are (they probably aren't) and with zero emotional investment (harder to do than say, for most people).

"The hookup culture narrative has fed into this culture of trying to pretend we have no feelings about the people that we have sex with," Friedman says.

In general, I recommend people think less about how much sex they're having compared to everyone else and focus on whether they're personally fulfilled with what they're having. There's a hefty amount of unstated pressure to go out and have more sex, so you can catch up with all the sex everyone else around you is definitely having. In turn, some men go out and aggressively pursue women in the ways they learn from fairy tales, and it's not leading to fairytale endings. One response to this reality is to bemoan the state of things. Another is to use the conversations that have resulted from the #MeToo movement to figure out what you actually want—what kind of sex you'd like to be having, whom you'd like to have it with, how you'd like to build a relationship. You don't need to have sex with everything that moves or meet any sex quotas.

"Generally, there is a gratitude in me for the awareness we, as men, have been afforded by this moment," Clint says.

Through Schmider's and Clint's eyes, there's a lot of freedom that can come with the opportunity to self-inquire right now.

So be gentle with yourself.

DO MEN STILL HAVE TO PAY
FOR DATES NOW THAT WE'RE ALL EQUAL?

I get asked this question a lot. Like, *a lot* a lot. During interviews for this book, especially, the moment I mentioned the word "dating" the male interviewees would almost immediately ask, "DO I STILL HAVE TO PAY FOR DATES?"

I have some theories as to why they did. First of all, this is a perfect example of how traditional notions of male and female gender roles are being called into question. The way you think about who pays might have been something you were raised to do from childhood, so you never questioned it, right? Plenty of people who have otherwise really progressive ideas about gender expectations hold legacy opinions on men paying for dates that they couldn't really explain to me. One of the men I spoke to, Murray, has really given this some thought.

MURRAY, 32

I have been on dates with women who have told me during the date their progressive views and ideals, which revolve around feminism and equality. And at the end of the date they expect for me to pay for the date. I have discussed this with women I dated and female friends, and the notion that a guy is supposed to pay seems to be entrenched into our culture. Now, if we take a longer, systemic view on it, though, for me this is the patriarchal system men have built over centuries biting modern men in the ass; the notion that the man plans and pays for the date, and the woman goes where he has planned, has restricted female agency.

Modern women have been taught that relinquishing their agency and being taken care of is an indicator that the man is worth dating. So, I don't like that women expect guys to pay. But before just blaming females as hypocrites, we need to look at why they feel this way.

Murray's dates, who seem very feminist in most areas, for some reason want to hold up this traditional gender role. Is that wrong? Here's a recurring theme in this book: there's no right answer!

No expert can tell you, "Oh, men always have to pay," or "Men and women should split it down the middle," or "Couples should calculate their earnings and pay for the percentage each makes down to the cent." The fact of the matter is that each person kind of needs to figure it out for themselves. What I'd like to do, instead of prescribing answers, is take a step back and figure out why we do the things we do. Then, armed with that knowledge, we can figure out how we want to approach things in the future.

For straight people who don't generally question their gender, this is all confusing. But queer communities have been trying to figure this stuff out forever. Jeffrey Marsh, a nonbinary Vine star and author of *How to Be You: Stop Trying to Be Someone Else and Start Living Your Life*, laughs when I ask about this question. "Straight people are just coming to terms with what queer people have been trying to figure out for centuries," they say. Get a grip!

Here's how a few men I spoke with approach this scenario:

"I will always pay for the date, not because I don't think of the woman I am with as equal, I was raised that way, to be a gentleman. . . ." —*Juan La Riva, 31*

"I don't think there's anything wrong with a woman paying for a date, but there's always that little twinge inside, or if I see my wife go to pay the check I feel almost like less of a man."
—*Stephan Badyna, 34*

"On the date I had recently I asked her, 'Can I buy your coffee?' instead of just insisting I buy it, you know?" —*Clint, 32*

"I expect equal contribution, according to means. Period."
—*Rich, 32*

A few years ago, dating guru Matthew Hussey posted a video[9] of one of his live events. Hussey has 1.7 million followers on YouTube, wrote the book *Get the Guy*, played the matchmaker on NBC's *Ready for Love*, and was the love expert on the *Today* show. Speaking to a group of women, the question of who should pay for dates came up. Hussey asked the group, "Who should pay?" and the group resoundingly answered "MAN!"

Hussey provocatively countered by suggesting that if the man has to pay for all the dates, shouldn't the woman have to have sex whenever he wants?

"No!" one woman called back.

Hussey made a face between bemusement and a smirk, and lifted his shoulders in a shrug.

"Where does this double standard come from?" he said. "I'm sorry, it's the reality. You can moan at it all you want, but the moment you say to a guy you have to fucking pay for my time, you're saying this relationship isn't equal. 'This relationship isn't equal. My time is worth more than yours, so you should pay for it.' I wonder what paradigm that sets up."

Hussey goes on to tell the mostly female audience that if they go on dates and don't offer to pay their own share, then the women weren't raised correctly. And then in the next sentence he says, "But if you go on a date and he doesn't pay—he wasn't taught right!"

He explains that women should offer to pay for what they can afford. It's when women don't offer to pay or there's the expectation that men pay that men feel used, Hussey says. This video has been uploaded multiple times with a view count totaling nearly 50 million, by the way. And the comments span the cross section of opinions you'd expect.

"When everyone's pushing for equality between genders then why would guys feel it's fair for some women to pick and choose what should be equal and what shouldn't be," writes Thomas.

"I am a quality woman in my 30s and I WOULD NOT EXPECT a man to pay for dates! Why should he?? He isn't my father/keeper," writes Katie.

On the flip side, Larry wrote, "I am old school. When I have lunch or dinner with a woman, it is just instinct for me to pick up the tab because 1) to prevent any awkwardness 2) when she agreed to have a meal with me the pleasure of the company is all mine 3) I believe a gentleman would do no less."

As Dr. Helen Fisher points out, we're in a time of tremendous transition. The shift from an old-school mode of thought to the new one comes with honestly just a lot of confusion. Baked into these pimply growing pains is a very real conversation about wealth and financial independence. Think again of the history of dating. Historically, wealth was transferred through the male line. When lower-income and immigrant women first hit the workforce in the early 1900s, the belief was that they were there to supplement the income of the men in their lives: their fathers, husbands, and brothers. As such, managers used this as an excuse to pay their female workers much less than men. Women made less than 50 percent of what the men in their positions made, writes Moira Weigel. And, she says, this is how it developed that men became expected to pay for dates. From *Labor of Love*, Weigel quotes a young woman who was living in a boardinghouse in the New York City neighborhood of Hell's Kitchen talking to a social worker in 1915. "If I had to buy all my meals I'd never get along," the young woman says.

The idea of men paying for dates sprouted from the idea that women should be financially dependent on men. Things have improved considerably, but there's still a 20-cent-per-dollar gender pay gap. (That's for all races. Black women, however, earn 65 cents per dollar earned by white men. It's 58 cents on the dollar for Latinx women.)[10] So, on the one hand, if you pay for dates, you're tacitly participating in a system that doesn't value women as much as it does men. But on the other hand, if you split things down the middle, you're asking someone who might make 20 percent less than you on average to meet you halfway. You're damned if you do, damned if you don't.

It's a deeply complicated topic, admits Arielle Egozi, the founder of Other Agency, a creative agency bringing diversity and representation to media and advertising. She also writes *Salon*'s nongendered sex and love advice column and has a popular Instagram account, @ladysavaj, that talks about sex education and gender equality. Do you see paying for dates as a nice gesture? Or do you see it as transactional? That it implies forthcoming sexual favors? If you think that you paying gives you power and leverage in the relationship, "[t]hat's bullshit," Egozi says. "If someone is wanting to pay because they are trying to even the scales because they recognize that women get paid less, then that is one thing. But if you're going into this like, 'I'm the man and my ego is offended if a woman pays' or, again, you think you're owed something at the end," then that's a problem. In other words, check your motivations.

This may go without saying, but this scenario is complicated, so take some time to figure out what *you* think about it. Then be able to explain what you believe and why—and talk about it with your dates. For instance, maybe you want an extremely equitable relationship, but also want to acknowledge the gender pay gap. Maybe you say, "Hey, I'll get the first two dates, but after that I'd like to split checks." This is awkward. We don't like to discuss this stuff with early dates. But maybe we should. It's an opportunity to figure out quickly if you want the same things.

"If you don't want to live in a world where you have to pay for someone's meal because they have a different body part than you, then don't create that world," Colin Adamo, the creator of *Hooking Up & Staying Hooked*, says.

In other words, don't date someone who doesn't share your values.

Dating has always been weird and awkward and full of fumbling, and now that generational shifts are calling into question the ideas that underpin relationships between men and women, it feels even more treacherous. As I've said before, men are spooked! The very idea of the masculine roles of pursuing and persistence doesn't hold up as well as it once did. But this is a chance to figure out what your relational needs are and find someone who can help meet them. It can be a relationship built on mutual pursuit.

One clear-cut example of all of this is in deciding who pays for dates. Traditionally this has been the man's role, going all the way back to the invention of dating. How *you* decide to do it will be personal, but again, it's a chance to communicate what you want from a partner and find someone who fits that.

Great. So by now you are an expert dater. Let's talk about sex, shall we?

Chapter 2
SEX

The incident happened eight years ago. But it's been fresh on Mitch's mind for the past two years since conversations about #MeToo hit the mainstream.

Mitch is a thirty-two-year-old systems coordinator in Washington, D.C. In 2011, he met a woman he really liked. Let's call her Kendra. They'd hung out as friends, but he was interested in more, so for New Year's Eve he invited Kendra to come out with him and some other friends. They all went dancing, the ball dropped, and then he invited some people back to his place to continue the festivities. Just Kendra and one other guy friend joined. They had a couple of more drinks.

As things started to wind down, the guy friend said he was going to take off. It was way past midnight at this point. After some discussion of subways and cabs, it was decided that Kendra would spend the night because she lived far away and didn't feel safe transiting to her part of town alone at this time of night—remember, this is before any-one knew about Uber.

"Oh wow! It's on!" Mitch thought at the time.

Mitch gets into bed and Kendra says, "I'm going to put on some pajamas." So she goes and changes into pajamas, but then gets into bed next to him. He makes a move to start fooling around and she says, "No. Stop." He stops for a couple of minutes . . . But then he makes another move that really upsets Kendra. "I was pretty aggressively trying to take her panties off and trying to initi-ate sexual contact," he recalls. In his intoxicated state, he's not one hundred percent clear on what was going through his head, but he thinks it prob-ably had something to do with certain beliefs he subconsciously held like "All women say no at first" and "Why would she say no if she's in bed with me?"

Very alarmed and distressed, Kendra gets out of bed immediately and goes to sleep on the couch.

Mitch tells me he's always been somewhat of a late bloomer and thinks he misread the cues, or subconsciously dismissed the cues. He's been haunted by it for eight years.

However, the story Mitch reached out to share with me is anything but unique to him.

WHO HASN'T HAD A HOOKUP LIKE AZIZ ANSARI?

Why would a woman get into bed if she didn't want to have sex? And do women often say no at first when they really mean yes? Why is sex and hooking up so fraught with seemingly confusing gray areas? These questions all predate the mainstream #MeToo movement, and maybe next to stories of rape and sexual assault at the hands of powerful men like Harvey Weinstein and Bill Cosby, they may hardly seem to fit to you. Case in point: Aziz Ansari.

Ansari's story is a #MeToo Rorschach test—meaning people's reactions to it seem to represent their larger underlying feelings about sex and the current conversation about the movement. You probably became aware of Aziz Ansari from his lovable, ridiculous character Tom Haverford in the comedy *Parks and Recreation*. From there Ansari developed his self-deprecating, charming nerd humor in stand-up specials. He talked about feeling like an outsider as a brown boy from a first-generation Indian-American family in South Carolina, and he talked openly about his nice-guy attempts that often fell flat with his dates.

Then in 2015, Aziz landed an original series on Netflix called *Master of None*, which he co-created, co-wrote, and starred in. You got the feeling that the main character Ansari played was very much based on Ansari himself—a relatable nice guy just trying to make it in New York City with women, his career, his parents, and friends. That same year, he coauthored a book with sociologist Eric Klinenberg entitled *Modern Romance: An Investigation*, which thoroughly explored the history of dating and the current climate and implications of online dating. I've personally cited this book several times over my years of reporting and thought of Ansari's tone as thoughtful, self-deprecating, and genuine. Basically, Aziz had long seemed like a classic "good guy"—and that he was educated about romance.

So, in early 2018, when Babe.net published a first-person story with the headline "I Went on a Date with Aziz Ansari. It Turned into the Worst Night of My Life,"[1] many people thought, "Oh no. Not him too."

The story recounted a twenty-two-year-old woman's date with Ansari, during which they went to an oyster place in New York City and then back to his apartment, where he began making out with and undressing her within minutes. According to the woman, he repeatedly stuck his fingers in her mouth and around her crotch, and he repeatedly tried to have sex with her. The woman asked him repeatedly to slow down and said she was uncomfortable. He seemed to understand and suggested they sit on the couch. That's when, she says, he pointed at his crotch and gestured for her to go down on him. When he tried to make another move, she said no and that she was uncomfortable. He suggested they chill with clothes on and watch *Seinfeld*. He aggressively kissed her again, trying to take off her pants, so she stood up and went to her phone in the kitchen. He called her an Uber, and she went home with tears in her eyes in the back of the car.

The next day, he texted her that it was fun to meet her. "Last night might've been fun for you, but it wasn't for me," she responded, according to the author of the Babe.net article. "You ignored clear nonverbal cues; you kept going with advances." She added: "I want to make sure you're aware so maybe the next girl doesn't have to cry on the ride home."

I hope you also agree that your hookups should absolutely not cry on the Uber back.

Sex, sexual experiences, and hookups should be mutually pleasurable. They should be hot, fun, and maybe even romantic interactions. But, the truth is: For a lot of us, they're awkward and uncomfortable because they're fueled by a hotbed of insecurities, miscommunications, one-upmanship and competition, and game theory.

"Think about it this way. For a driver's license, you had to take a class for half a year, take six courses, practice tests, et cetera. That's a lot of preparation!" Colin Adamo, the creator of *Hooking Up & Staying Hooked*, says. "And yet, for sex and hooking up, which are the foundation of what we build our whole society on . . . no one teaches you this stuff!" Adamo isn't defending Ansari here. He's just commenting on the absurdity that such critical aspects of our intimate lives get left in the bumbling hands of us imperfect humans, with our sole guidance coming from movies, porn videos, maybe an older sibling or kids at school, and—I guess if you're lucky—a sex ed class from likely your home economics or gym teacher.

I've spent a lot of time reporting on topics like this—topics that we're supposed to have figured out as adults, though truthfully no one really has. So let's look at how this could have gone instead—for Ansari, for Mitch, and maybe for you, too.

"Not every pussy is the same," Michelle Hope says. "You cannot have sex with every vagina the way you had sex with the last vagina."

Hope is a sexologist with a master's degree in human development and a particular interest in the intersections of sexuality with race, class, gender, and sexual orientation. She's facilitated workshops all over the country with a wide range of organizations you may have heard of—from the Los Angeles Police Department to the Harlem Children's Zone. You can find her as a guest on Vice News and *The Breakfast Club*. She makes me laugh with her line "Sexuality doesn't start at puberty—[it's] from the womb to the tomb, baby."

"So, yes, it is important to ask what your partner likes, and it's also important that your partner is comfortable telling you what they like," she says.

Seems obvious, no? But how many words do you exchange over the course of any sexual experience? What would that look like in practice? Oh, I've definitely got you covered there.

"Let's say you have your hand on her inner thigh, and the next move would naturally be to touch her between the legs," Dominick Quartuccio says.

Listen, just a warning, we're about to get technical here.

"Now, you don't know if she's ready for that, so before you go there you can just circle your hand around the inner thigh, and you could feel if she's tense," he says. "Like is the muscle tense, or is it relaxed?"

We heard from Quartuccio in the first chapter. He's the co-host of the *Man Amongst Men* podcast and regularly talks to "high-performing" men about doing inner work.

"The next cue is to pause for a gentle moment and to look her deep in the eyes with a big smile on your face, or a sign of lust, or whatever look you want to give in that moment, and to ask her, 'Are you ready? Or would you like me to stay here?' And then watch how she responds," he says. "If she's having difficulty responding to it, then okay, let's just hang out here."

What's important is that when you ask that question, you can genuinely feel like it's okay if she says no. Because she'll sense it if you're pressuring her, he says.

"In that space, what's communicated is 'it's all good.' Allowing her to feel like 'no' is completely welcome. That is the thing that a lot of women have shared with me," he says. "If you can make her feel that a 'no' is going to be completely welcomed, and when she does say 'no' you give them a big smile like, thank you for sharing." And then, "If that changes, you'll know because she'll take your hand and put it right between her legs when she's ready."

ROUND OF APPLAUSE!!!

Quartuccio also touches upon an idea that came up consistently with the conversations I had with men: the idea of slowing down—tuning in to your partner and listening to nonverbal cues. This is also what Ansari's date says he ignored.

"When we want to think about active listening it's not just hearing the words a woman speaks, it's hearing the tone in which she speaks them. It's interpreting her body language. Active consent can be wordless if there's understanding between people," Jack Summers tells me.

Jack Summers looks like a man's man. He's tall and in excellent shape and owns an alcohol manufacturing company in Brooklyn. He also speaks publicly about social and human rights, feminism, and race. But in a previous life, he hosted a blog called "F*cking in Brooklyn" that chronicled his adventures and sexcapades after divorcing his wife in his mid-twenties, finding himself, and healing a broken heart. Summers then went on to be the editorial director at the Good Men Project, a website and blog with nearly 1 million followers on Facebook.

"If it's about her pleasure first and not yours, then it's an easy thing to go, 'Well, this might make me feel good but this isn't really working for her, so I shouldn't do this.' Meaning, put your partner's pleasure before your own. What an idea!" he says. "Too many times the idea of the man means being aggressive, and that means ignoring signs that a woman is not actively consenting to something—or overriding those signs because it was what you wanted. I think the thing that helps us avoid situations like that is decentering maleness."

This can be a challenge for some. It's hard to pay attention and listen when you've got a boner! (So I'm told.) To be safe, especially if you are with a new partner with whom you don't have a deep level of emotional intimacy, stick to clear, verbal communication. In the same way that anal sex is not beginner sex, nonverbal consent is not first-time hookup material.

"The thing that always comes up in stories of sexual assault that are in the gray areas is that some men will say, 'But some women don't like it when you ask!'" says Lux Alptraum, author of *Faking It: The Lies Women Tell About Sex—and the Truths They Reveal*. "And I always say, 'Why are we privileging the people who aren't comfortable communicating? If you can't communicate your desires, then you don't get to have sex that night!'"

Obviously Ansari didn't heed this advice. Honestly, neither did a solid 50 percent (if not more) of my own high school, college, or, let's be real, post-college hookups. This situation is so common that most people just think of it as "a bad date" or even "a normal date." As I said, the reactions to the Ansari story reveal a lot of what our own expectations for sex and hooking up are—and this isn't split down the line by gender with women siding with the woman in the story and men siding with Aziz. No, definitely not.

"After reading the story, I felt he completely mishandled the circumstance," Javier, a thirty-three-year-old first-generation Mexican-American husband and father from Florida told me in an email. "I believe he should've been more aware of her hesitation, and should not have pressured her thereafter."

When I asked Javier what makes him sympathize with the woman's perspective, he continued, "It certainly reminds me of an incident my wife experienced in her early twenties. She was dating a guy, and one night when they were kissing and touching, he kept insisting they have sex. Despite her continuously saying no, he kept insisting they just do it. It got to the point where she gave in to him in order to appease him."

Now, this could make you think that anyone who had first- or secondhand experience of a situation like the woman in Ansari's or Mitch's stories would align with Javier's opinion. But I didn't find that to be the case. Many of the people I interviewed for the book feel like these stories did the #MeToo movement a disservice. They argue that the #MeToo movement is critical but should be reserved for the stories of egregious acts of sexual violence. These people fear that the more glaring acts of violence and mistreatment would subsequently be taken less seriously when lumped in with conversations about what several people have dismissed as simply a "bad date."

"You would hear, 'Harvey *and* Aziz?! Holy fuck—there's a big difference!'" Dominick Quartuccio tells me of his private clients and men's group participants.

And this sentiment comes from women and men alike.

An open letter[2] from a hundred French activitists, academics, and actresses, including famed French actress Catherine Deneuve, denounced the #MeToo movement because of stories like Ansari's. "Rape is a crime, but insistent or clumsy flirting is not an offense, nor is gallantry macho aggression," it reads. Furthering that sentiment, multiple women I spoke with told me, "Women have to take responsibility for their own actions. Should he have stopped when she said 'no'? Yes. But why didn't she leave?" One thirty-three-year-old public school teacher in the Bronx told me, "That's half of my sexual experiences in my twenties—I'm not crying about it! Some of this #MeToo stuff is going too far."

After having these conversations, I often had the thought *Okay, yes, maybe this kind of thing happens all the time. But should it?* Because I think we probably can and should do better. Unraveling the reasons that sexual experiences between men and women can be so fraught with complications is … well, complicated. But one of the more glaring underlying problems is that, traditionally, women have been viewed as the gatekeepers of sex, which is a belief based on the inaccurate, unfair, and harmful assumption that men always want sex and it's women's job to decide if they can have it or not.

"At a very early age the paradigm or the dynamic is set up where women are gatekeepers and guys are just trying to persist as much as they possibly can. They're trying to get as far as a woman will let them go. And I don't know if that's ever explicitly taught. It's just kind of the expectation. You know as a guy you just want to get it in," Quartuccio says. "It sets up this really wonky dynamic that gets played out as we become older. I've talked to women about this, and they're like, 'Dude, it's fucking exhausting.'"

Now, do women really want less sex? I hate this question, so I'm just gonna hold my hand up as one of the womenfolk who enjoy sex and say—No, absolutely not. Women like sex, too. Moving on.

I've always found this narrative that women don't like sex as much as men to be inaccurate, and also unhelpful. I've spoken to plenty of women during my years of reporting who want just as much sex as their male partners, and plenty of women who have wanted *way more* sex than their male partners. And for the women I've spoken to who aren't as interested in sex as their male counterparts, I think this claim that it's just the "way things are" reinforces an idea that women don't and shouldn't enjoy sex—something I think we can all agree is patently false.

"One thing I'd like people to figure out is [that] men fall in love just as often, [and] they fall in love faster," Dr. Helen Fisher, the biological anthropologist who works with Match.com, says. "I'd like the world to know that men are just as romantic and women are just as sexual."

Does that hold up biologically as well?

"Psychologists have been cataloging male and female behavioral differences for half a century or more, and most of them are quite modest," Dr. Lise Eliot, the neuroscientist, says. "But when you get to things like sexuality, like masturbation frequency, you do tend to see bigger sex differences."

She suggests that most of those are learned and absorbed far before puberty, from what she calls "chastity cultures."

"As far as what your actual raw physiological sex drive is, I don't have a good sense of whether there's a huge difference there. I suspect there is some difference between males and females," Dr. Eliot says. "Certainly, testosterone promotes sex drive. Of course, men have higher levels on average after puberty, but, interestingly, of the hormones, female testosterone does go up at puberty—and that is much more strongly associated with girls' sex drive than, say, estrogen changes."

It's generally accepted among researchers that there are more social factors at play than biological in this realm.

"Across cultures women are more cautious about sex than men, for the simple reason that women can get pregnant," Dr. Eliot says.

But outside of the fear of pregnancy, which birth control has largely helped us manage, women face a range of social consequences after sex that men traditionally don't.

"This is something for men to be aware of," Quartuccio tells men at his public talks. "Physically, she may be turned on, too, but she has to also consider her reputation, has to consider whether or not you're a trustworthy guy, or you're going to go and slander her, or slut-shame her, or tell your buddies about it—all of that's going on in her mind as she's determining whether or not to go further. And, for most guys, the only thought is: Can I proceed?"

This gets us to the real problem with thinking of women as the gatekeepers and men as just "wanting to proceed." It sets up the idea that sex is something to be taken from another person— a transactional experience rather than a joint and mutually enjoyable activity.

"It sets up a dynamic where sex is almost seen as adversarial," says Lux Alptraum. "That matters a lot because if you're just seeing sex as a path to your own orgasm, then it doesn't really matter how the other person feels about things. But if it's an activity that's about everyone having fun together, your decision-making is going to be very different."

I spoke with several men for whom this sounded familiar, and I was grateful to those who were so earnest, by the way. I know this can be hard to admit, because mediocre sex or not, societal pressure is still geared toward transactional sex. I can tell you that because, well, I live in society—and also it's what many men told me. One of them was Chris, a salesman from the Midwest who is in his early thirties and works at a major tech company.

"I'll be the first one to tell you, like in my early twenties, I'm not necessarily happy or proud of how I acted," Chris says. "There's a sort of thing like intense pressure ... the sole purpose of going out is to bring a girl home."

When he was growing up, his relationship with women was "more like a feat, like a conquering-type thing. It was more like *obtain* rather than *build* a relationship—and have fun." When I straight up asked him if he saw women as people, he responded, "Uh, yeah ... but I would say I fell into the traps of—not necessarily dehumanization—but like it wasn't always cool to be into some-body. It was always better looked upon to be like, 'Oh, I didn't care anything about her.'" Chris says most of his friends were like this, and even to this day he knows the worst in his group is currently in counseling for this exact kind of behavior.

You think of your mom as a person. You see your sister as a person. But someone you want to have sex with? They may be just a vagina.

This brings us back to Mitch's story: the guy who aggressively pursued his female friend on New Year's Eve. "Oh yeah," he told me. "You're always thinking about the end goal. Not just making the first move, but how to start the conversation to make sure that you make the first move and push it towards sex." So when Mitch heard the Aziz Ansari story, he says, "My reaction was, 'Shit, I've definitely come razor close to an experience like this . . .' In fact, it sounds like he did have that exact situation, except that for Mitch, he was able to talk through the situation with Kendra and his story never made it onto a news site.

If this sounds like any of your sexual experiences, sex educa-tor Lux Alptraum recommends reframing sex in your mind. Think about sex as you would think about having dinner out with a friend, she says. You both want each other to enjoy the meal—not have one person need to eat faster than the other; not that you both have to order the same thing. And maybe even if you don't enjoy the same things, there's a discussion and a compromise. For example, maybe you do sushi one time for one person because it's their favorite food, and then next time you do Mexican food because that's the other person's favorite. So brilliant.

Alptraum also points to the fact that some men, whether consciously or unconsciously, feel like they need to use tricks to get women to sleep with them or they won't get laid: a little more alcohol, or a promise of deeper emotional intimacy than you really want, or, as was the case with Mitch, repeated aggressive advances. Sure, maybe your numbers go down initially if you abandon those tactics, but the result is that you'd end up having *better* sex because it would be with people who *really* wanted to have sex with you!

Alptraum tweeted[3] about this idea late in 2018, writing:

> **@LuxAlptraum**
> Straight men would have so much more sex if they just treated their casual sex partners with the tiniest modicum of respect and human decency.

A couple of folks echoed her sentiment with responses such as the following:

> **@corintxt**
> I have tried to explain this many times to fellow men and somehow it doesn't sink in.

> **@PoMoGhoul**
> It is honestly like a killer Lifehack I'm surprised more men haven't discovered.

What would your sex life look like if every time you hooked up, you were thinking about the experience just a little less in terms of your own orgasm and a little more in terms of your partner's pleasure? Or, as Lux frames it, "What if—instead of seeing sex as something you had to take from someone—you saw it as something you had to create together?" she asks.

While I was writing this chapter, an Argentine sex toy company called Tulipán launched a new buzz product: a condom that requires four hands to open the packaging. Meaning, in order to use the condom, both partners would need to be involved. CBS News hailed the product as "making [a] powerful statement about consent."[4] Others . . . disagreed.

> **@MoiraDonegan**
> Frankly it's incredibly optimistic of them to think that the kind of man who doesn't care about consent *does* want to use a condom.

The four-handed condom may settle in the graveyard next to other widely panned products with the well-intentioned aim to promote consent. Like consent apps.

On *The Chappelle Show*,[5] you may remember a skit with Dave Chappelle and actress Rashida Jones. Jones and Chappelle are on the bed hooking up when he pauses to roll over and pull out a piece of paper. "What's this?" she asks. "The Love Contract," the narrator replies. "Just initial there for oral ..." Chappelle says to Jones, side-eyeing her hopefully. "Oral?" she asks. "I'ma do you too!" he says. So she signs. "And then just initial there if you decline anal," he says, looking at her real hopefully. "No, no, no, it's not going down," she says, initialing her name.

The audience is giggling at this point because, yeah, it's so awkward and unrealistic to make someone sign a contract about this kind of stuff. Then the skit ends with the narrator saying, "The Love Contract—because you'd hate to catch a beef for something you know you didn't do."[6]

What's the problem with an idea like this? It may get two people to talk openly about the kind of sexual activity they're about to have. And isn't that what we want? Of course. But it's a lot more complicated than that, says sex educator Haylin Belay, the founder of Sex Ed for All.

A consent contract is similar to a form you sign "like you do with a doctor," she says. "Like, 'This is all the things that we're going to do today.' It's essentially like, 'Now you're releasing me from liability if you leave this interaction feeling bad. Right?' That is what the legal model of consent means. So that is so not sexy. That's not how human beings have sex," she says.

It's that idea of what is legal versus not legal that underlies the whole conversation about sex, Aziz Ansari, and #MeToo. Belay, Alptraum, and Adamo all maintain that average people struggle because we think of consent in terms of what is legal and not legal.

By the way, this is a major theme in this book: We like straightforward rules, black and white lists, do this/don't do that commands. But life is not always that clear-cut. Welcome to the gray areas, my friends.

"I think the Aziz Ansari story struck a chord with people because it describes a type of sexual violence that is captured in the spectrum of sexual violence," Belay says. "That falls short of what a lot of people, of all genders, have been taught to consider 'bad.' Because we've been working with this really black-and-white definition of consent." It might help to give just a quick historical recap of the history of consent. For a long time, women were viewed as property, passed from father to husband. So sexual violence, Belay explains, "was thought of as property crime, usually a violation against the man who owned her. So, either her husband or her father." This means that if a woman was raped or sexually assaulted, the law saw the crime as an offense against the woman's father or husband, and not her, since she was technically property.

"One of the reasons why marital rape was conceptually beyond understanding during that time," Belay explains, is that "if we're thinking about this as a property crime, how can you know if I destroy my own TV? Who am I going to sue?" It's exactly because of this history that we've been conditioned to think of consent in terms of what is legal and what isn't—and that is a major problem, says Belay.

"If I am talking about consent, I'm talking about a very specific ongoing process between two people. That is more about empathy and mutual care than it is about strict legality," Belay says. "If I'm in a situation where I sign that contract and then something happens and I leave that interaction feeling bad and I feel violated, that person now has a document saying that I gave them permission to do whatever they did to me. And that again is not how consent works." The fact is that consent is ridiculously confusing for a lot of us, namely because we think of consent in terms strictly in the legal sense. Instead, it might help to think of consent in terms of empathy.

A lot of our confusion stems from our fundamental discomfort when it comes to talking about sex. Most people are super uncomfortable articulating their sexual desires—especially with the people they're having sex with! There's so much shame and stigma associated with sexual acts and fantasies, for all genders. Since everyone has their own definition of what they like and what feels good, navigating this conversation can be like walking through a minefield. So instead of navigating it, society has traditionally encouraged guys to just make moves without asking or checking in, lest they seem unsure of themselves.

I don't know what episode of *Seinfeld* Ansari and his date watched, but one of my favorites is the episode[7] when George Costanza tries to combine his three favorite things: sex, watching TV, and pastrami sandwiches. Naturally, he tries to do this without telling his sexual partner. While under the covers, he discreetly opens his nightstand drawer to pull out a pastrami sandwich. "Spicy mustard!" he says, and she giggles, thinking he's talking to her. "Oh ho ho ho, you're hot tonight!" When he puts in an earpiece to hear the TV, she rips off the covers and asks, "George? What are you doing?"

"I got greedy," George later tells Jerry. "I flew too close to the sun on the wings of pastrami."

The point is that sex is definitely a both-hands-on-the-steering-wheel type of situation, people. You want to be present, open, communicative, and intent on both of you having a good experience. If you're not, you're going to risk leaving behind a series of unsatisfied lovers crying during the Uber ride home, which some may see as just a "bad date," but I know we can do better.

WHAT IF SOMETHING GOES WRONG?

Okay, so the worst has happened, and you, like Mitch, realize you fucked up. What do you do?

Let's get two things out of the way. The first is that what I'm talking about here is not the kind of thing that could land you in jail. That kind of situation is more complex than we have time for in these pages—although some of the lessons we're about to talk about still apply. However, we can all agree that there are a lot of lower-level shitty things that can happen during sex that won't necessarily put you behind bars, but are still really harmful to others. We know from many areas of the law that just because something isn't illegal doesn't mean you should do it.

The second thing is that I'm also not talking about false accusations.

This one comes up in nearly every conversation I have about this topic. When it comes to false accusations, I think the most helpful thing to do is start with the numbers.

According to RAINN (the Rape, Abuse, and Incest National Network),[8] one of the leading national organizations in the sexual assault prevention space: One in every six women in America has experienced an attempted or completed rape.[9] One in every thirty-three men in America has experienced an attempted or completed sexual assault.[10] For every 1,000 rapes, 995 perpetrators will not go to jail. That's because only 230 of the 1,000 rapes will be reported to police. That means three out of four go unreported. Of those reported, only 46 will lead to an arrest. Of those arrested, only nine cases will be referred to prosecutors. Only five of those will lead to a felony conviction—and not even all of those five convictions will lead to incarceration.[11]

The reason so few cases are reported is obvious to anyone who watched the hearings of then Supreme Court nominee Brett Kavanaugh, anyone who knows someone who has been sexually assaulted (and statistically, you do), or anyone who's watched pretty much any Lifetime movie. Survivors of sexual assault are often treated terribly by their community and the legal process. Forced to relive a traumatic experience over and over again, frequently disbelieved and made to be the villain, survivors often have a very low incentive to report a sexual assault crime—and because of the widely understood terrible treatment that sexual assault survivors receive when they report, the incentive to report a false sexual assault crime is also very low.

The oft-cited figure of false accusations is 5 percent. But according to Joanne Belknap, a sociologist, criminologist, and professor at the University of Colorado Boulder who spoke with *New York* magazine's sister site *The Cut*[12] in 2018—the 5 percent number, already low, is actually much, much lower. At the very highest, Belknap says that only 10 percent of rapes are reported, meaning that the 5 percent of false accusations can apply only to the 10 percent reported, which would put the rate of false accusations among rapes committed in this country at 0.5 percent, according to Belknap.

That's half of 1 percent.

So if you're a numbers person and you're worried about men, says Jaclyn Friedman, author of *Unscrewed: Women, Sex, Power, and How to Stop Letting the System Screw Us All*, stand with sexual assault survivors. Even as a man, you're more likely to be the victim of assault than the victim of false allegations.

Friedman is direct in a way that she doesn't care if she hurts your feelings. Like the title of her book would imply, she's spoken nationally about issues of gender and sex.

"When we talk about taking care of each other and making sure your behavior isn't harming anyone and taking women more seriously as people," she says, "if that makes you worry about yourself . . . I think that's good information for you to be aware of."

What she really hears when someone frets about false accusations is, "If women have more power, if we're to believe women more and take them seriously, then women's voices are going to be amplified and taken as true. Then I would feel that my power will be reduced and that makes me feel vulnerable."

One in six women will be sexually assaulted, and yet most women continue to operate in the world without assuming all men will assault them. That being said, I wouldn't worry too much about women falsely accusing you.

But let's get back to the original question: What do you do if you've engaged in some less-than-consensual sex? What if you were way too aggressive pulling off someone's panties, like Mitch?

Alptraum's advice on this is pretty straightforward: "Everyone fucks up, right? Own that."

Once again, she recommends thinking of it like you would think of a situation where you've hurt a friend's feelings. Validate the person's hurt and ask them what you can do going forward. And if someone blows you up on social media? Again, she says, think about it like it was a friend who texted you to say you had hurt their feelings. You would talk to them and apologize, right? "Just because it's sex doesn't mean that you cannot admit you did something wrong," she says.

I heard from many of the men I talked to that they're torn—on the one hand they really empathize with the messages behind #MeToo. And on the other, they're feeling really defensive because it seems like all men are being nailed to the wall right now. So, who in their right mind would own up to even a small misstep when it feels like that could get you pegged as the next Aziz Ansari—with the third season of his show canceled, basically banished from the public eye?

"The apology is just step one," Friedman says. "The short answer to this is that you have to actually seek redemption. It's not just a period of time passing—you have to do the penance and do the work." In other words, it's not like you can just sit at home for a year and then start dating again and expect everything to be chill.

"Repentance is hard work," Friedman says. "You have to figure out what it was in you that allowed you to do that harm and then shift that inside of you. How do you atone? Does your victim need some sort of compensation? If not, how do you do better for the larger community?"

Here's the thing—Aziz didn't die. In fact, as of April 2019, he's back with a new nationwide comedy tour—and he's actually come to see the silver lining on the situation. While he was preparing for the upcoming tour back in February, he stood in front of a live audience to test some of his jokes and reflected on the experience of the past year.

"There were times I felt really upset and humiliated and embarrassed, and ultimately I just felt terrible this person felt this way," he said, according to *Vulture*.[13] "But you know, after a year, how I feel about it is, I hope it was a step forward. It made me think about a lot, and I hope I've become a better person."

Vulture also reported that a friend told Ansari that the friend had been rethinking every date he'd been on in light of Ansari's public reckoning. "If that has made not just me but other guys think about this, and just be more thoughtful and aware and willing to go that extra mile, and make sure someone else is comfortable in that moment, that's a good thing," Ansari said.

I don't think I'm reaching here when I say there is a large opportunity to learn from this cultural reckoning and move forward on a large scale, but for us to do that, we have to own our mistakes on an individual level.

Mitch is glad he could do just that. The morning after the incident with the woman, he immediately went out to the living room and sincerely, genuinely apologized for what he had done. He took responsibility for his actions and listened to her feelings on the night before. This might not have been enough for all women, but the conversation made such an impact on Kendra that they're now actually quite good friends, Mitch tells me.

"I own my personal responsibility for that night and I'm also thankful for the fact that we were able to conduct ourselves with open, honest, and authentic communication," Mitch says.

Sex is confusing and weird. It's an intimate, vulnerable act, and everyone does it and likes it differently. And yet, despite this, we hardly ever talk it through, even with sexual partners.

You can avoid a lot of headaches and heartaches—and probably have way better sex!—by just articulating what you want and earnestly asking your partner. Maybe skip the nonverbal communication with first-time hookups and stick to making everything explicit.

If you do fuck up, own it. Admit your fault, apologize for it, and then do the work of figuring out how you got to that point. Change whatever needs to be changed inside you so that it doesn't happen again. It seems basic, but because we never teach men or women to reflect on their sexual motivations, we just don't do it. However, when you're solid on what your personal motivations are, your own behavior will feel a lot less anxiety-provoking.

And that will truly help you when it comes to how you conduct yourself personally in the professional sphere.

Chapter 3
WORK

Alejandro oversees a department of ten people within a larger company of three hundred. Recently, his CEO scheduled a meeting with him. When Alejandro arrived, the head of Human Resources was sitting with the CEO. That's never a good sign . . .

Alejandro was, as he told me, completely shocked to find out that he'd received two separate verbal sexual harassment complaints for making inappropriate comments with sexual innuendo. They wouldn't tell him what he said and they wouldn't tell him whom he had offended, citing the need to protect the employees' anonymity.

As far as he could tell, there was no formal investigation conducted and he was handed a letter stating this was his first and final warning. They didn't offer him any training so he could make sure he didn't make the same mistakes again. Another complaint would result in termination and loss of stock options. In Alejandro's mind, his entire career, which he's worked so hard for, could be over in a blink of an eye—and he considers himself a good guy! Later that day, he went home and didn't sleep for a few nights, trying to figure out what he possibly could have said.

Alejandro has stopped going into the physical office so much, choosing to work remotely instead. He doesn't go to off-site work functions and considers everything he says in the presence of a coworker, particularly if they're a woman. For the most part, he's concerned about the equity he holds in the company. One more ding and his life's work could disappear.

"Any woman can lodge any anonymous complaint against any male and that guy's gonna get crucified over it. Your career's just been irreversibly impacted and it creates a very scary environment for men, like holy shit," he says. "And it's unfortunate because I think it's going to have a regressive effect where men don't feel safe talking to women or building social connections with women, which we know are really important for the progression in an organization and for promotions."

He's still stumped by what he possibly could have said.

SHOULD YOU HAVE TO WATCH EVERY DAMN WORD THAT COMES OUT OF YOUR MOUTH?

Alejandro's story seems to be the encapsulation of many of your worst nightmares—you're just walking around, doing your job, and next thing you know, you've been unfairly accused. Boom. Career over.

I heard from many of you that #MeToo has you walking on eggshells, scared to say or do anything that'll land you in hot water because the new rules of engagement are really unclear. This seems to be particularly true in the workplace. In fact, more than any other chapter, this one might be the touchiest, so if this is how you feel, you're not alone.

According to the Pew Research Center, more than half of Americans said recent developments have made it more confusing for men to interact with women in the workplace. LeanIn.org[1] also did a survey in 2019 that I frankly found pretty alarming:

- Sixty percent of male managers say they're uncomfortable participating in a common work activity with a woman, such as mentoring, working alone, or socializing together. That's a major jump from a year ago, when the number was 32 percent.
- Thirty-six percent of men surveyed said they avoided these types of activities—and more specifically, they avoided mentoring or socializing with a woman—because they "were nervous" about how it might appear to others.
- Senior men report being six times more likely to hesitate to have a work dinner with a junior-level woman than with a junior-level man, and nine times more likely to hesitate to travel for work with a junior-level woman.

It's clear that there is a lot of fear right now about a "witch hunt" mentality in the workplace. According to a *Glamour* and *GQ* survey,[2] a third of men (ages 18–55) are personally worried about being wrongly accused of sexual harassment at work. The number gets a lot bigger for those making six-figure incomes.

I think these fears have the potential to obfuscate other real areas for improving the workplace for both women and men, so let's examine them—starting with Alejandro. Forget touching, forget drinks and inappropriate behavior or a hookup even—this was just a couple of passing comments.

"Right now, don't say anything without thinking carefully about every word that comes out of your mouth because one wrong word can be a career-limiting or -ending one," Alejandro says. "One slip, one stupid comment that you didn't think through, and it can be completely misconstrued. And that's the scary part."

It's left Alejandro to wonder, *Do I have to watch everything that comes out of my mouth now? What can I even say or not say?* It's an interesting question, so let's consider what others think about it.

There are people who specialize in making workplace cultures and environments safe for employees. They're called human resources professionals. One is Sarah Morgan. She's a senior human resources director for an international organization. Not for nothing, but Sarah Morgan is the most candid human resources professional I've ever spoken to.

To her, the very question of "What can't I say?" is the wrong place to start.

"What's frustrated me in the process is—and this is typical of workplace behavior in general—people want rules and not guidelines," she says. "*I want a rule that tells me to do this and not that*—which is how people end up in uniforms. Now I'm finding that people want rules surrounding interactions between women and men in the workplace to absolve them from potential liability. And it's like no, that's not how this is going to work. There is no list of rules." She points out that she can't pull out a stopwatch and time everyone's hugs to make sure they're under 2.3 seconds, or whatever timing would be friendly but not inappropriate.

"From a human resources perspective, there's absolutely what's lawful and unlawful, and I get that," Morgan says. "But with relationships—and that's what you have at work, you know, the vast majority of the time—sure, there's liability involved in how people interact, but the vast majority of what you're doing is just normal human interaction. The law doesn't really dictate that. Power dynamics dictate that." Those are the same power dynamics that mean you earn 20 cents more per dollar than your white female colleagues, 35 cents more than your black female colleagues, and 42 cents more than your Latina colleagues, according to the Pew Research Center.

Part of Morgan's job is to look at where and how people are represented in different areas of the company. One project she's working on is examining the pay discrepancy of the telemarketing team at the company she works at. Commissions are involved in the pay structure of this team, and across the board the men perform better than the women. When they looked at why that might be, they heard repeated feedback that potential clients were turned off by the higher-pitched voices of the female sales associates. (This phenomenon of people not liking the sound of women's voices is so common that the popular podcast *This American Life* explored the trend in an episode. The segment revealed the disproportionate amount of negative feedback that female radio reporters receive about their voices, versus male colleagues.)[3]

One way to look at the situation is to hold up your hands, sigh, and grumble about how the world is sexist, but Morgan and her team tried to take a more nuanced view. Could they fix the internalized sexism of someone who won't make a purchase because a higher-pitched voice called them? Nope. But, there are a bunch of other areas to look at.

First, they scoured the pay inequality data for areas to improve. "What can we do to support those individuals to make sure that we level that playing field and give them the opportunity to be able to achieve, despite the external factors that are making it more difficult for them?" she asked. That might mean supplying additional training for those who want it.

Next, they looked at the world years down the road. There's a pay discrepancy at her company now, in 2019, so what can they do to help alleviate that a decade from now? In two decades? She started looking at how they recruit. "We've got to be actively looking to diversify our talent, now," Morgan says. "We have to also say, 'Okay, this pipeline is clogged. And what can we do to make sure this pipeline is more equitable?'" Morgan has steered her recruiting team to look at communities and organizations that support women to tap talent for her company.

This may feel like it's drifted a long way from #MeToo, but

Morgan sees it as all part of the same conversation. Bouncing your ideas off people from a variety of genders and races helps shape them in ways that might not expose your blind spots if you're talking to only one group.

"Any workplace that lacks gender diversity is going to have #MeToo issues," Morgan says. Now, if I imagined Sarah Morgan and Alejandro in the same conversation, I think Alejandro would likely reply, exasperatedly, that he still doesn't even know what he said. He doesn't know whom he offended or why, so how's he supposed to fix that? Alejandro was very clear with me that he still wants women to be able to make anonymous complaints. He's thought a lot about the gender pay gap. He was raised by a single mother and cares about women and equality. But now he's worried that he's on the receiving end of "fake news," as he called it, or an embellished complaint from a miscommunication with a stuffy female employee or an HR director he's butted heads with in the past.

"We have this knee-jerk reaction to shoot first and ask questions later. That's a dangerous place to be. And that's kind of where we are right now," he says. "I don't know the state of where we are with regard to how you protect women or men who are feeling unsafe or in a hostile work environment. How do you protect them while at the same time not allowing for baseless witch hunts to take place? All it takes is one—one instance where someone misunderstands, and that's the game changer," Alejandro says.

The fear of false accusations rippled through almost every conversation I had about this book, so I think it bears repeating (as we discussed in the previous chapter) that the numbers suggest the risk of false allegations is very low. In the workplace specifically, these numbers are confirmed anecdotally by professionals. In 2018 the Employment Law Alliance, a global human resources legal solutions firm, conducted a survey of nearly four hundred employers from all fifty states. The survey found that harassment claims were rarely fabricated, with only 6 percent of respondents indicating "more often than not" that claims were false.[4]

"I can tell you in my fifteen years working in HR, I have never had somebody come to me that did not believe that the situation they went through was legitimate enough to come forward," Victorio Milan says. Milan is a human resources professional who has worked in the retail, restaurant, and now nonprofit industries. "Nobody ever lied. They may not have had all the facts, or the context by which they were coming forward. It might not have been as bad as they thought, but they did not do it because they wanted to get back at somebody."

When Alejandro complained to his CEO that he'd have to watch every single thing that comes out of his mouth, the CEO, also a man, was sympathetic. "It's just a really shitty time to be a man," Alejandro remembers his CEO saying to him. "I have to watch every single word that comes out of my mouth," Alejandro repeats to me.

Despite Alejandro's frustration, thinking before you start talking is actually sound advice for professionals in any setting—and it's something women are already *quite* used to doing.

"We all have a responsibility for how we show up, the energy we bring, the way we make people feel in our presence," Morgan says. "I don't think #MeToo changes that. I think it brings a different level of attention to it, and men haven't had to pay attention to that before. So it's uncomfortable for them, because suddenly now they have to be mindful."

Like Sarah Morgan, I heard from some people that there was a whole new level of awareness happening that feels uncomfortable, but I don't necessarily view being uncomfortable as a bad thing. The thing is, the workplace as it was originally designed was never intended for women, and, TBH, maybe it hasn't gotten the upgrade it needs to accommodate everyone, of every gender, in healthy ways.

Let's rewind back to World War II, when there was a huge shift in the workplace. In 1940, about a quarter of women worked outside the home in the United States, mostly for low pay, doing tradition-ally "feminine" jobs like secretarial work. But after men increas-ingly started shipping off to war, women began replacing them at their jobs. Some 5 million women joined the workforce in the next five years, according to Ellen Carol DuBois and Lynn Dumenil, authors of *Through Women's Eyes: An American History with Docu-ments*. By 1950, a third of women over fourteen held jobs outside the home, and half of them were married—and once they started making more money, they wanted to keep their jobs. Seventy-five percent reported wanting to continue working after the war, even though many were laid off from factory jobs to make room for the returning male veterans.[5]

The millions of new women now at the office and in factories were entering a male-dominated sphere—places designed for and by men. When women joined them, the ingrained assumption was that they were not to be taken seriously as workers. As we discussed in the dating chapter, right from the get-go women were paid less than men. As another illustration, take the expression "MRS de-gree." This concept popped up in the 1940s to describe women who attended college, but were supposed to be looking for a marriage certificate rather than a diploma. Take also the various plots in the show *Mad Men*, where women—pigeonholed in support roles and viewed mostly in terms of their physical appearance—were often trying to find ways to be seen as the competent and talented work-ers they were.

"It wasn't like now where it's just like, 'Oh, only one woman in the boardroom,' but it was also this understanding that secre-taries were sex objects and that secretaries were hired to be male entertainment," says Lux Alptraum, the author of *Faking It: The Lies Women Tell About Sex—and the Truths They Reveal*. "And so there is that history that women have been fighting with and grappling with."

Now, listen, you may be like, *This does not apply to me. A) that was decades ago, and B) I don't see my female colleagues like sex objects, I see them as people.* Good! But I heard some stories that just make it clear all of this is more insidious than we like to admit.

"I said to her that she better watch it or she might get fat and her husband might leave her. . . . She told me as we were walking away that 'she was too good on her knees for him to ever leave her.' We both just laughed. . . . Well, an hour or so later, we were in the break room and she had one of those e-cigarettes and was smoking it. I said, 'That must be your famous technique to keep him happy.' I wish I had not said that but it was in a room full of people who say things and show things on their phones [that are] much worse. She laughed and that was it, so I thought. I was called in on my day off and they started an investigation on what happened. I was told it was inexcusable." —*Luke, lost his job in November 2017*

"#MeToo, what took you so long? I remember being in a corporate meeting back in the late eighties with seven to eight men and two women. . . . Senior leadership was bad-mouthing both women and discussing their bodies like it was some sort of dessert. . . . I held a resentment against one person, which eventually led to my dismissal." —*Calvin, 52*

If this time period is teaching us anything, it's to look more closely at ourselves and our motivations—not only in ways to make sure you avoid getting dinged by HR, but also to make your office a better place for everyone employed there.

How? I'm glad you asked.

SHOULD MEN MENTOR WOMEN?

Murray works in international relations at an international governing body. He started in his field as an unpaid intern, hustling just to get a paid job. When he finally broke through into a salaried job with power, he was determined to help those coming up behind him, he told me. So, fast-forward to today: One of his interns is really standing out from the pack, and she's showing immense promise. Wanting to nurture her talent and bring her up in the ranks, he's starting to meet with her one-on-one to help her with some of the more difficult assignments he's tasked her with. Despite always meeting on-site, and in conference rooms with glass walls, the rumor mill still started almost immediately.

"Nothing happened between us, but some people at the office automatically assumed that either we were already sleeping together or that the only reason I mentored her was because I wanted to sleep with her," Murray says.

Murray heard the typical locker room jokes and comments from other male colleagues. It kind of sticks in his craw that the worst ribbing came from men who had actually hit on her, something Murray thinks is inappropriate. But eventually the gossip got so bad that his boss, also a man, confronted him about it. He explained to his boss that his intentions are purely professional.

This situation is bad for everyone. It's awkward for the intern who found out that her male colleagues have been talking about her in a sexual way, which is unprofessional and unacceptable, even though Murray tells me that she and he just laugh and shrug it off together. On his end, Murray is rightfully pissed that he had to explain to his boss that the intern is talented and worth mentoring, something he'd obviously never have to do if the intern was a man, he says.

This harks back to the idea that men and women can't interact without sex being the common currency, which is an idea that no self-examined person can really believe.

So, you're here to help, right? And one way people can help others' careers is by mentoring them.

"Statistics show that men are still predominantly at the positions of power," Danielle Moss, an attorney who specializes in labor and employment law at the international law firm Proskauer Rose, says. "We as a society have to normalize the concept of male mentorship toward others. And I say that not just about women, but across demographics—racial, religious, sexual orientation, et cetera. If we're going to shift the dynamics of power, those in power have to start mentoring not just women but everybody who's different from them."

Murray does think #MeToo has been good for the corporate world. "I think this is creating a bit more of a buffer, as in people are more scared," Murray says. "And that's a good thing." But let's be honest here: if you're still iffy about what you're allowed to say out loud in the workplace, navigating a mentor relationship with a woman can be even more troubling.

You know who actually takes this concern to the hilt? Vice President Mike Pence.

The vice president of the United States of America refuses to dine alone with women or attend events that serve alcohol without his wife, Karen.[6] Twitter mocked him pretty mercilessly for this. "Mike Pence Asks Waiter To Remove Mrs. Butterworth From Table Until Wife Arrives," a headline in the *Onion* read. But despite the public condemnations, some people found themselves quietly wondering if maybe Pence might be onto something. Now that the #MeToo movement has gone mainstream, surely there was some merit to avoiding even a semblance of wrongdoing.

In 2018, Bloomberg[7] interviewed thirty senior executives from law firms, banks, hedge funds, and private equity firms who are cautiously considering similar rules to the one Pence has. "A manager in infrastructure investing said he won't meet with female employees in rooms without windows anymore; he also keeps his distance in elevators. A late-40-something in private equity said he has a new rule, established on the advice of his wife, an attorney: no business dinner with a woman 35 or younger," the article reported. One called hiring a woman nowadays "an unknown risk." These men aren't even remotely alone. From that LeanIn.org survey, we know that half of male managers are uncomfortable doing common work activities with a woman.

I want you to imagine the woman Murray mentored. In pretty much every civilization since humans started recording history, one gender has held the majority of the positions of power in industry and government.

That gender is, spoiler alert, not women.

And for a similar length of time (all of recorded history), the main way to advance in industry or government has been to sit down and chat with those in positions of power, learning from them and developing relationships with them and getting mentored. If men can't mentor women, Murray's coworker may imagine herself jumping and leaping, trying to grasp a ladder as the men on the floor above her pull it up after them, out of her reach.

As of 2018[8], only twenty-four female CEOs led Fortune 500 companies, down from the previous year's thirty-two (a record high). According to the Institute for Women's Policy Research,[9] it will take until 2059 before American women reach pay parity with men. For black women, it'll be 2119.

WTF.

On a global scale, the World Economic Forum[10] predicted in 2016 that it will take 170 years to reach gender parity in the workplace. Then, two years later, in 2018, after the #MeToo movement gathered steam, it projected parity in 202 years.

Holy hell. That's a long time for Murray's coworker to wait. And it's apparently getting longer. One of the only solutions to speeding that process up is people in power, namely men, going out of their way to mentor those who traditionally don't have power.

Danielle Moss advises her clients to use "good judgment." That's lawyer-speak for cut the crap and, yes, it may not be as much fun, but leveling up is not always fun. Also, it's work. "For example," says Moss, "taking a female colleague out for a business lunch near the office—without alcohol and with a logical beginning and end— limits the potential for misunderstandings, whereas a late-night dinner all the way downtown, away from the office, may cause risk or misunderstandings."

Keep the communication mode professional as well. "For example," she says, "professional emails during normal business hours are preferred to intimate text messages or social media messages outside normal working hours." Honestly, everyone (woman or man) would appreciate their bosses keeping communications to working hours and not on personal devices.

Moss also points to companies themselves that should take on some heavy lifting and make things less awkward for employees. She has in mind the formalization of mentorship programs by companies to eliminate the potential for malicious gossip. "If everyone knows that various male or female leaders have been specifically assigned to others as 'mentors,' the hope is that any misplaced chatter about that mentorship or time spent between those individuals is anything but aboveboard," she says.

This is an interesting idea. I'm curious to know if Murray's renowned international diplomacy organization will start formalizing mentorship programs.

WHEN IS IT OKAY TO SLEEP WITH
OR MAKE A MOVE ON A COWORKER, IF EVER?

DON, 32

After the live taping ended at 10 p.m. on Mondays, Don would finish up whatever work absolutely needed to be done for the next day and then take the crew out to get drunk.

Don was a lead producer on the show, in his late twenties, chubby, and living off the adrenaline of live TV. The crew was small and ragtag. Recently, they had been trying to settle on a director. The most talented one at the network was too busy. The second most experienced didn't gel with the rest of the team, so they promoted an assistant director, Maggie. She'd been doing the job for several weeks, but the team planned to demote her when the original choice became available again.

One Monday, the crew ended up at a dive club after the show where you could dance until the sun came up. Don and Maggie danced together all night, and then moved to his apartment, a couple of blocks away, at 4 a.m. When Don made his move on his balcony, Maggie sputtered, "Haha, no." Don's feelings were hurt. He felt grumpy and told her to call an Uber.

In the morning he realized what a big mistake he had made. They already had plans in the works to replace Maggie the next week and now he, her boss, had made a move and she'd rejected him. He knew how this was going to look. Why hadn't this occurred to him before?

When he got into work, Don pulled another producer, Paul, aside, and without explaining the full situation, recused himself from the decision. It would be solely Paul's decision what to do. Paul was a little confused, since they'd already agreed to replace Maggie, and decided to go ahead with that plan.

This was the first time Don had ever had to consider his conduct as a boss, or even imagine why managers shouldn't hit on subordinates in the first place. But now he was thinking about a potential lawsuit, and trying to create a paper trail.

Some of you guys might have felt like Don before, waking up hungover, trying to figure out what's happening. But after #MeToo, you may be like, *Well, does this completely take interoffice hookups off the table? Is there still room for romance at work?* Before I dive into what you should or shouldn't be doing, let's figure out what people are already doing.

According to a 2015 study by Approved Index, 65 percent of people who work in an office have been involved in at least one workplace romance. Just about half have had two or more romances. *Business Insider* found similar results in 2013. According to their poll, 54 percent of people have slept with a coworker. (Half of those hookups happened at the office itself. So, uh, maybe make sure your janitor is well compensated.) Eighty-five percent of respondents to that *Business Insider* survey thought it should be okay to sleep with a coworker. So, it seems that, by and large, Americans think this is acceptable.

Some of these instances are just hookups, but a significant number led to longer-term relationships. A CareerBuilder poll[11] in 2014 showed that 37 percent of people have dated a coworker, and 30 percent of those relationships led to marriage. In fact, a lot of people find their spouse at work. A 2017 study by ReportLinker[12] says 15 percent of all relationships that led to marriage began at work. The number shifts by year and study, but basically there are three main ways people meet each other today: through friends, while online, and at work.

However, having an office romance is still not totally accepted in the public eye. According to that Harris poll, a third of office romances try to keep it on the down low. A quarter were with a boss or superior. When the romance sputters, it can get dicey. Five percent of those who have had an office romance left that job once it turned sour.

But the majority of the people I talked to felt like, in general, as long as both were on equal footing at work, you're good to go.

> "If neither of you are in a relationship, and it's consensual, go for it. Makes day-to-day work a little more fun and interesting." —*Ronaldo, 30*

> "If your job is completely meaningless and there is NO differential in power, if it's a side hustle, and you won't share with other colleagues, or brag to other colleagues, then go for it. Otherwise, NO. There are seven billion people on the planet. Everyone loves Jim and Pam from *The Office* but it leads to more problems than good." —*Colin Adamo,* Hooking Up and Staying Hooked *founder*

This starts to hint at what Don was pushing up against: the way power interacts with sex in the workplace. What happens when you dump your boss, who has the power to fire you? How should women handle it when someone with a lot of power at the company asks for sex? I do not have the answer to these messy questions, so the advice I got from the professionals is: If there's a power dynamic, don't do it. It's just not worth the risk.

Don told me he now won't even consider making a move on anyone whose role is further down the chain of command. How must Maggie have felt, rejecting her boss and getting demoted from that team the next week? Spoiler alert: probably awful. And honestly, I wonder if this had happened now instead of five years ago, would Don have found himself in HR the next morning?

It raises the question, *When does your office flirt become something inappropriate?*

It can be difficult to pin down what exactly entails sexual harassment. Workplace abuses are rarely as obvious as the Harvey Weinstein situation. When asked directly, "Have you experienced sexual harassment by a man?" by YouGov in 2017, about 60 percent of American women said yes. A nonprofit called Stop Street Harassment polled a bigger sample and asked more specific questions in 2018. More than three-fourths of women said they had been verbally sexually harassed. Over half reported unwelcome sexual touching, and 38 percent of this harassment happened at work. I think anyone would agree this last figure is entirely too high. It doesn't seem like a stretch to say that most people—men, women, anyone—would think we can do a lot better. But how do we make public spaces, and in particular workplaces, safer for everyone? One tip is to treat all of your female colleagues like you do your male colleagues. Alejandro, for one, is already considering where he interacts with coworkers, by meeting only at work during work hours.

So, let's talk happy hours. There's a bunch of research on how happy hours help build relationships at work, improve morale, and so on. People who like each other and are working together make most things at a job better. Drinking with coworkers well into the night also tends to lead to some questionable situations— and those who don't drink can often feel left out of vital work chat. Does that mean we should cancel all happy hours? No, of course not. But if you're the manager making those decisions, maybe explore other situations to supplement them. Family picnics? Lunchtime yoga? It's handy to have an array of ways for employees to hang out so no one group is ostracized or afraid to show up. The solutions will probably be as varied as there are numbers of offices.

"Business is done wherever knowledge is being shared and wherever opportunities are being created," Danielle Moss, the attorney at Proskauer Rose, says. "That is where everyone should have an equal shot." Often that isn't at the office.

With this in mind, let's consider Billy Graham, the famous preacher who helped found the evangelical movement in the United States. In 1948 he and his male staff drafted the Modesto Manifesto (named after the California city, not a weird riff on modesty). It included some commendable things, like not lying about crowd sizes and being financially accountable, as they tried to avoid the scandals that had plagued many of the evangelists at the time. But one of the pillars was that no man from the group would be alone with any woman who didn't happen to be his wife—and Graham took it seriously. In fact, Graham took it so seriously that he made Mike Pence look like Caligula.

"From that day on, I did not travel, meet, or eat alone with a woman other than my wife," he wrote on page 128 of his autobiography, *Just As I Am: The Autobiography of Billy Graham*.[13] He reportedly broke the rule only once, when Hillary Clinton convinced him to meet her for lunch at the Capitol Hotel, a public location.

"When my grandfather would check into a hotel, a man would go inside the room and look under the bed and in the closets," Will Graham, his grandson, told the *New Yorker*. "What they were afraid of was that someone had snuck into the room, like a naked lady with a photographer, and she'd jump into his arms and he'd take a picture, and they'd frame my granddaddy."

Decades later, when Billy Graham was in his nineties and his health was failing, he still stuck to what had come to be called the Billy Graham Rule.

"He's got 24-hour nursing care at home," Will Graham told the *New Yorker* in 2017. "There are always two nurses, for accountability purposes."

Even on his deathbed, with professionals specifically trained in an area where he needed help, Graham continued to see these women within a sexual context.

Albert Burneko, a writer at the sports news website Deadspin, wrote a rebuttal to this type of thinking:[14] "[F]or these men—at least in their imaginations—the chute leading from an overcooked burger at Chili's to, like, an entire secret second family, is wide, straight, steep, and absolutely drenched in WD-40. *Who knows what might happen if we sit down to mozzarella sticks together! It's all out of my hands from that point on!*"

Burneko's summary is used for comical purposes here, but you get the drift. And while Graham's approach may seem extreme, we know from the poll numbers that others are quietly considering somewhat similar protocols. This is not only ill-advised, it may also be illegal.

"You are essentially trading gender harassment for gender discrimination," Danielle Moss says. "If you're not doing one-on-one meetings with women, don't do any one-on-one meetings with men." Plain and simple.

So, is it okay to sleep with a coworker?

There's no hard-and-fast rule here. It's one thing to have two coworkers make eyes at each other and start a relationship over lunchroom salads and cubicle flirtation. But it's another thing to remember the history of gendered power dynamics in your industry and how that's affecting how you see coworkers.

"It's like, well, is it two people who happen to work with each other who genuinely feel a spark and want to pursue a relationship?" Alptraum says. "Or is it someone feeling entitled to the other person because of their gender? Is it somebody feeling like you are a woman in the workplace and therefore you are here for my entertainment and you are here because you want to be perceived sexually?"

Alptraum suggests just going slow. You've got the rest of your life to deal with this—you might as well make sure you're being clear and communicating early, even if it's just a casual fling. Because if things go poorly, you're still stuck bumping into each other walking out of the bathroom, or cc'ing each other on office party invites. It would suck to cause someone to leave their job because of a spoiled office romance with you. Just a simple (though perhaps tough) conversation at the front end could prevent a lot of messiness later on.

Oh, and maybe don't try to sleep with someone you know you're about to demote. Just a friendly tip.

Instead of considering these tips as an infringement on your rights, think of them as better work practices—or at least a chance to reconsider how and why we do things the way we do, and how to tweak the system to improve it for everyone involved. None of this is comfortable or easy, but the #MeToo movement suggests it's necessary. Where men have to get comfortable is in messing up. When something doesn't land well, apologize immediately, try to do better in the future, and move on.

"If you treat another individual as a human being first and foremost, you tend not to think about how you're going to be misinterpreted," Milan says. "And if you are, you have a conversation that allows you to acknowledge your mistake and figure out how to fix the mistake and move forward as professionals."

You're not perfect, and no one expects you to be. But we do expect you to try.

It might help to shift focus. So instead of fretting over what you can and can't do, spend more time thinking about how to create a more equitable workplace where people from different backgrounds can thrive.

"I've never met a man who has created awareness around this topic and not come away from it saying, 'I want to be different and I want to do better,'" Sarah Morgan says. "The sooner we can get men to have awareness, the sooner we can get to the 'how do I help?'"

Chapter 4
MONEY

At twenty-eight, fresh out of rehab and with legal charges pending, Brian quit his job and took a 50 percent pay cut to become a craftsman. It was the only way to get healthy, to move beyond the opioids and alcoholism that had fueled his life as a "successful," six-figure-salary art director.

Brian was, in his words, a "short brown immigrant kid" who had "always been super sensitive." At fourteen he turned to substances to cope with feelings of inadequacy. When he finally got clean, he met a woman who was a successful surgeon. She saw through all of his bullshit, valued him, and helped him rebuild a life.

"I can say with absolute confidence that without her support during those first few years I would have relapsed and OD'd," Brian says.

She also made 6.5 times as much as he did and that didn't matter to her. "I am not exaggerating when I say that how much money I made was utterly meaningless to her," Brian says. "She always respected my work ethic, but as long as I continued to contribute to our home equally, both financially and domestically, she really couldn't care less about how much more I made or saved."

He remembers her repeatedly saying that she loved him for him, not because of a job. But the money thing bugged him.

When other men learned he was dating a surgeon who was making bank, he got mixed responses.

"A lot of guys [in general] were of the 'Oh, dude, that's so awesome that she's a surgeon. You guys will live comfortably' perspective, which could not possibly be further away from how I felt myself," Brian says. "I never ever even remotely considered her as a means of financial support or security at any point. It stressed me out."

Once she wanted to take a week off to go to Iceland. In his former job, Brian could have dropped everything and gone with her. But craftsman Brian? It would take major long-term planning to afford a trip like that.

They kept their finances separate, and Brian insisted on paying half of everything. Even though she didn't care that he made less money, and most of his friends didn't care, Brian started hustling to make more money. He picked up freelance work on the side, often working seventy-five hours a week "to try and bridge that gap."

"Ironically, in doing so, it actually ended up being the catalyst that slowly broke apart our relationship," Brian says. "I was so focused on trying to make more money that I stopped being a great partner. I was always working, and we grew apart over time."

After three years, they broke up. He still regrets it. If he could go back, he'd do it all differently.

"I will always love her," he says. "Because the first two years were amazing. Truly the best of my life. And I know it was me obsessing about making more money that drove us apart over time. As much as that hurts to admit."

WHAT IF SHE MAKES MORE THAN YOU?

Men want to be providers.

That's not me saying that. Well, I am also saying that, but it's not *just* me. Pretty much every single man I interviewed for this book said it as well, and so did Dr. Helen Fisher, the biological anthropologist. But she also clarified this statement.

"I wouldn't say '*the* provider,' I would say '*a* provider,'" she says.

Dr. Fisher writes a lot about pair bonding, and she points out that only 3 percent of mammals pair up to rear their young. Humans are part of that 3 percent. "Monogamy evolved 4.4 million years ago, and, with that, males not only had to provide for themselves, but they helped to provide for a female with the evolution of pair bonding."

Dr. Fisher describes hunter-gatherer times as "dual income" because while the men hunted, the women gathered—thus making them both contributors. However, men came back with a kill only one out of four times. It was actually up to the women to provide in between. Because of that, meat was considered a luxury item.

"About 20 percent of the daily fare was meat provided by men. If they caught something big everybody might relax for three weeks as they all shared in it," Dr. Fisher says. "But men were providers of the luxury items. Women were the providers of the daily fare, which were fruits and vegetables and berries and maybe even small mammals."

This was how things worked for a couple of million years. Men hunted. Women gathered. A dual-income family was pretty much the only way to do it. Then some people decided to start planning what they would be gathering ahead of time. They planted crops and built farms, and from that sprouted agrarian societies. With this new normal, the dual-income norm shifted to one with men in the more central role, according to Dr. Fisher.

Men tended to move the rocks. Men tended to cut down the trees and till the land. Men sold the produce at the market—and brought back money. Women would pick, weed, prune, cook, and birth. They couldn't roam to gather anymore, since someone had to look after the farm, so that's when we evolved the idea that a woman's place is in the home—and the idea that man is the "sole provider."

"The idea of a principal provider emerges from agrarian past in the last ten thousand years—not the way the human males and females are built, not the way we lived for millions of years in hunter-gatherer society," Dr. Fisher says.

This new norm held firm throughout the industrial revolution, until women started to enter the workforce. So now, instead of farms, we have these things called "jobs," where we sit in rolling chairs at cubicles and click buttons on a computer until we get to go home. Then someone in a cubicle-with-actual-walls, usually called an office, gives us paper tender that we can trade for goods and services. This is called money.

"Money is the way we survive," Dr. Fisher says. "The new survival mechanism is to have money." Aside from the pay wage gap, money likes men and women equally—meaning the modern shift toward both men and women contributing financially to a household is actually reverting back to the dual-income partnership model.

Among married couples with children, 59 percent are dual-income.[1] This is becoming the norm. Dr. Fisher maintains that it's built into both men and women to want to provide—that it's just human nature—and now a modern society where women participate in the workforce and even outearn male partners is returning to a norm where both sexes can do that.

"Right now, right in front of our eyes, we are shedding the concept of the sole provider," Dr. Fisher says. "The double-income family is once again the rule."

That brings us to today. A survey by A Woman's Nation[2] found that 63 percent of men are "very comfortable" with a partner who works. In fact, Dr. Fisher tells me that "over fifty percent of men want a partner who not only has a job, but has a career and is interested in her career." But what if her career or salary tops yours? A lot of us still have a holdover idea that the man is supposed to be in the driver's seat professionally, or at least financially. Although it killed him to admit it, Brian certainly wasn't in the driver's seat. If he were, he wouldn't have blown up the best relationship of his life.

Let's look at just how far along, statistically, we are with making the idea of "the provider" gender neutral. When it comes to gender and money, the prevailing issue of our time seems to be the gender pay gap. This, it goes without saying, is unacceptable. But though critically important, that snapshot doesn't tell the whole story. Increasingly, men are on the decline financially. In 1950, 14 percent of men weren't working. Today that number is 31 percent. The unemployment rate for men is slightly higher than for women.[3] A portion of that is due to education: People with no high school diploma have almost three times the unemployment rate as those with a college degree. Since 2014, women have been earning more bachelor's degrees than men.[4] Women have been earning more master's degrees than men in the United States since 1981, and as of 2017 women between the ages of eighteen and twenty-four earned more than two-thirds of all master's degrees. They earn 80 percent of all doctoral degrees.[5]

This is part of the larger generational shift happening that we have to acknowledge.

"Our parents grew up in a totally different time, so some of the norms or conventional wisdom from their generation has seeped into our way of thinking even though they no longer make mathematical sense," Priya Malani, the cofounder of Stash Wealth, tells me.

Malani is a financial expert who has been invited to speak at Cornell, Harvard, New York University, Yelp, Twitter, Cole Haan,

IBM, Blue Apron, and more. She's Refinery29's resident financial expert. She spent most of her early career on Wall Street, where she quickly rose to the rank of vice president at Merrill Lynch, but came to realize that unless you have $10 million, no one is going to actually answer your questions about money. So she helped found Stash Wealth, "a financial planning firm for H.E.N.R.Y.s™ [High Earners, Not Rich Yet]," to help educate those in their twenties and thirties about making smart decisions with their money. (Full disclosure: I am trying my damnedest to be a H.E.N.R.Y. as a client of STASH myself.)

One of those generational holdovers she mentioned is the idea that you have to buy a house.

"We feel inadequate that we're not buying, because it's been very difficult for our generation to buy homes when we're paying off student loans," Malani says. "So, gosh, are we throwing money away by renting? We feel so guilty about this, but mathematically, it's absolutely not true."

She pointed to the work of Robert J. Shiller, who won the Nobel Prize in economic science in 2013. According to his research, in the past 126 years, housing prices outside big cities have risen 0.37 percent when controlled for inflation.[6] "So basically they've not been an investment at all," Malani says. "Again, this is outside of bubble markets." But still!

Part of this generational shift has to do with college debt. In 2018, 69 percent of college students took out loans, and they graduated owing about $30,000 on average. Only 14 percent of their parents took out student loans.[7] On the whole, Americans owe $1.56 trillion in student loan debt. That's about half a trillion dollars more than our combined credit card debt. Millennials, specifically, graduated from college with a mountain of debt, just in time for the 2007–08 financial crisis to make sure there were no jobs available to help pay off that debt.

The nature of jobs has changed as well. The concept of the full-time job with benefits is evaporating. During President Obama's administration, for example, 94 percent of the 10 million jobs created were part-time or contract.[8] By 2014, one in three Americans was a freelancer. That's about 42 million people.[9]

"Millennials deserve more credit—both from themselves and from others—for their mindfulness when it comes to money and their lives," Andrew Plepler, the global head of environmental, social, and governance at Bank of America, says. "Let's not forget, many millennials entered the workforce during the most severe economic downturn since the Great Depression. However, they seem to have weathered the storm quite admirably."[10]

Ultimately, the idea that you go to college, get a good job with benefits, and then buy a house is outdated. Despite all this, and despite millennials getting made fun of for eating avocado toast, young people are out there hustling and patching together a living—and particularly women.

It's within this cultural context that I want to introduce you to a concept known as "financial feminism."

"We are not going to be equal with men until we are financially equal," Ellevest cofounder (and a renowned legend on Wall Street) Sallie Krawcheck says on the *Forbes* podcast *Hiding in the Bathroom*.[11] (Someone give whoever named that podcast an award.)

All throughout my childhood, my mother wanted me to be financially literate and financially independent, and she really impressed this upon me, I think, because I'm a woman. I remember her giving me a copy of famed financial expert Suze Orman's book *Women & Money* when I was sixteen, and I remember at the time being like, "Ugh, no." But I got the message loud and clear—and I don't think I'm the only one. Being a smart woman means having your own source of income—it's an idea many of her generation imparted to their daughters.

Here's an interesting fact: it wasn't until 1974 that women were legally guaranteed the right to open a personal credit card. Before that, many banks required single women to bring along a man—a brother, a husband, a dad, whoever—with them to cosign for a line of credit. Even Hillary Clinton has a story about being denied a credit card in the seventies. She was told to use her husband's instead.

Financial feminism is the idea that money is a key ingredient in the liberation of women. It's a term I first heard when I became a fan of Farnoosh Torabi. Torabi is a personal financial expert, the host of the *So Money* podcast, and the former host of a prime-time CNBC series called *Follow the Leader.* She also has written three books about personal finance, the latest of which is titled *When She Makes More: 10 Rules for Breadwinning Women.*

"We have to think of ourselves first," Torabi says. "It seems selfish, but you have to put your own oxygen mask on first and then you can take care of everybody else."[12]

Torabi's new project, She Stacks, is a start-up aimed at financially empowering women through products and media content. Torabi's cofounder, Kindra Meyer, explained the catalyst behind the company. "After the election, like many women, we broke down and broke through," Meyer told the *New Yorker* in 2019.[13]

"We came to this conclusion that until women are financially literate and empowered around money, we'll never truly have equality."

And here's how this all comes back to #MeToo.

In 2018, financial guru Suze Orman came out of semiretirement to relaunch her famed book *Women & Money.*

"I started to realize the role that money plays in the #MeToo movement and everything," she said on a panel hosted by *Money* magazine in 2018, with Torabi as a co-panelist. "It is fabulous that women now are finding their voice and they're finally saying what's happened to them. And there isn't one of us, I'm positive, that it hasn't happened to—especially at my age, it's happened many times, but I had the power to say no."[14]

She had the power to say no because she was financially secure. In Orman's opinion, it's harder to reject the advances of your boss if you don't have enough saved for next month's rent. It's difficult to ignore a meeting with the Harvey Weinsteins if you haven't made it yet.

In other words, money is a huge way the power imbalance is tipped to allow abuses to happen to women.

"The subtitle of the book is to be strong, smart, and secure," Orman said. "It's my way of trying to say, 'Come on, ladies. This is the time that you now have a voice. Let's have a financial voice.'"

For many women, this push toward financial feminism comes in subtle and not-so-subtle forms. But it still doesn't smoothly fit in with traditional gender roles about finances. Torabi's book *When She Makes More* offers tips to women who earn more than their male partners, which is something Farnoosh can speak to personally.

"When a woman makes more than her man, the rules are totally different," writes Torabi. "The latest data shows that women under the age of 30 have higher median incomes than men in nearly every major city in the country. Of all married couples across all ages, 24% include a wife who earns more, versus a scant 6% in 1960."[15]

So in a sense, what we have happening in our culture at the moment is financial feminism butting up against some men's desire to provide. I think this is where most of the tension is coming from in Brian's story, and all the other men who told me about similar hang-ups. I had multiple men, who would otherwise describe themselves as forward-thinking and progressive, admit that they have a real issue not being the main breadwinner in a heterosexual relationship. And it surprised even them!

What do we do with that?

My mind always goes back to a *Fight Club* quote: "You are not your job. You're not how much money you have in the bank. You are not the car you drive. You're not the contents of your wallet. You are not your fucking khakis." It's important to separate the idea of someone's worth as a human being from their net worth.

"The same way that men are taught to think that sex is solely about their dicks, men are also taught to think that contributing to their household solely comes in [the form of] money, and they don't think about the million other things that are required to run a household," Lux Alptraum says. (You remember Alptraum by now, I hope. She wrote *Faking It: The Lies Women Tell About Sex—and the Truths They Reveal*.)

If you don't know this, it's a fault of modern society that hasn't caught up to the realization that there are many ways to be a provider! Think back to Dr. Helen Fisher describing a pre-agrarian time, when hunting, gathering, and rearing children were all part of providing. Or, for a slightly more modern take, listen to Kyle Wright, cofounder of Wright Wellness Center in New York City.

"Guys don't get asked, 'Hey, what makes you feel good about being a male partner in your relationship, or a man in general?'" Wright says.

Men are often told: make money, be tough, provide, protect. But there are many, many other ways to provide for a partner. For instance, let's look at Wright's life. He was a bartender for a decade. He put his wife, Rachel, through school so that she could become a psychotherapist. As a bartender, his clients would rib him about Rachel leaving him for a man with an equally advanced education. When I asked if that ever got to him, he told me he thought it was more a reflection of his patrons' insecurities, not his own. And when he wanted to transition out of bartending, she turned the tables and supported him.

"One of the reasons [men] would want to make more money, that I found, in relationships is [that] they want to be able to spoil their partners," Kyle says. But it's nice to enjoy being on the other end, too. He remembers a time when his high-earning wife bought him a rare bottle of expensive whiskey, his favorite kind. "That's the thing that having a financially independent partner gets to do for you, and I think that a lot of guys don't think about that."

Rachel supported Kyle for a few years as he dabbled in a few different careers. Eventually they realized they had the same calling and founded the Wright Wellness Center, to help people learn how to create and sustain long-term relationships.

"Guys still want to have the idea of 'I'm providing for my partner.' They still want to provide in some way," Kyle says. "We had a conversation when Rachel took over as the primary breadwinner about what I would provide to the relationship." For them, they decided that Kyle would keep the house in a way that when Rachel would come home, she would feel nurtured and taken care of. That included foot rubs, buying groceries and cooking dinner, doing the laundry (she still folds). Eventually it'll include changing diapers, he says. Sometimes other men would razz him about the pay disparity.

"I always figured when people would ask stuff like that, it's so much more telling about them than me. It's not my situation they're really worried about," Kyle says.

"So I'd ask the male clients who bring that up, if they have issues surround money, 'What is [your] real value [in the relationship]?'"

I talked to so many men who grappled with this question.

One of these men is Chris. His girlfriend got a stellar job in another city, so he quit his job and moved to be with her. (It helps, he said, that he had probably stayed in his old job a few years longer than he should have.) But the job hunt in a new city quickly got to him. He set his standards pretty high, and it took him a year to find work again.

"It's tough because I don't know if I feel the pressure as a man or if I just feel the pressure as one-half of the relationship," Chris says. "Especially when I moved, I felt a huge amount of guilt and pressure. It took me so long to struggle for a job. And I don't know if that came from a place of being able to contribute or provide as a man or just as the other adult in the relationship."

After a year of job hunting, Chris found seasonal work. Eventually he ended up taking a job at a popular tech company, and even though he isn't all that excited about the particular role, he says there's plenty of room for growth.

"Maybe I felt that more because there was never that doubt in my mind that I would be the person providing it all. Does that make sense?" Chris muses. "Like, I never really thought it was because I was a man, but traditionally relationships have a higher likelihood that the man is the number one provider and the woman isn't. So I guess that idea just never came into my mind, that I could be the not-providing person."

Chris was contributing in other ways, of course. When his girl-friend had major surgery, he took care of her, helping her to the bathroom for two weeks after. You can tell that experience of him being able to care for her means a lot to both of them. He also took over many of the household duties and ran errands, especially pick-ing up medicine so she wouldn't have to make a separate trip after the workday.

When I spoke to men from all over the country, and from a range of backgrounds, here's what they told me about earning less than their partners:

Jack Summers, 51

My dad was a jazz musician in the 1940s, toured with Louis Armstrong, Billie Holiday, Duke Ellington, etc. He sent money home, but Mom raised us. And Mom made it clear that there are other ways a man can contribute to a household than "being a good provider."

Dating women who made significantly more money than I did forced me to confront certain insecurities and freed me to focus on how I could contribute in other ways. I confronted these insecurities with honest communication with my partner: How I felt, what she needed in terms of support, whether or not she would view me as lesser if I were not the breadwinner.

I contributed by contributing financially and making sure she felt supported in her career, and taking responsibility for household chores: laundry, grocery shopping, cooking. And I paid for a cleaning service once a month.

Did I get ribbed from friends? They thought I had it made: beautiful, brilliant girlfriend with a lucrative career, who valued me not for my utility but for my humanity. They were jealous.

John, 33

I do think [because of] the fact that I have student loans and credit card debt, especially living in a capitalist society, I worry sometimes that I don't have anything to offer another person, and that's a concern of mine. . . . I lived with a woman, and I paid for everything. I ended up racking up credit card debt. It actually got to the point where I said, "I think we should split everything equally," and we ended up breaking up about a month later. I don't think the two things were related. . . . This might just have to do with me and my personality rather than the fact that I'm a man, in that I really like to dote on some-body and give them what they really want. If someone offered to pay, I was just very insistent and would act like I had more money than I did. In that way, relationships could be really hard for me.

Adam W, 37

I've been with my wife for twenty years (started as seniors in high school) and she's always outearned me—mostly due to how our career paths worked out, but I'll admit, it *really* bothered me for a while. We'd argue and I'd guilt her, and in hindsight it was a pretty stupid thing to be upset about. I know it was because of the family I grew up in.

It was very traditional, with Dad working eighty hours a week in an auto plant and Mom at home, doing the laundry, grocery shopping, gardening, and making sure dinner was ready for when Dad got home. My mom never "had" to work. She would get a job from time to time but it was never at my dad's direction. I felt our relationship/marriage should be the same way, but after a while I just became okay with it. I'm not sure what finally made me get over this stubborn fantasy of mine, but obviously we're better off because of it. We have three *very* active boys and I frequently find myself wishing I didn't have to work so I could better manage their schedules. Because I work from home I find myself striving to make sure dinner is ready for Mom when she gets home. I guess, in a way elements of that *Leave It to Beaver* upbringing I had are still there, just not in the way I imagined it!

Brian, 57

There have been times when she has earned more than me, and it has never bothered me. I looked at it as a team effort. She, on the other hand, has despised me when she had to be the primary breadwinner.

She wanted to be June Cleaver.

It would come up if she didn't feel I was pulling my weight or if we had an argument about spending on one thing or another. It was usually straightforward—"I don't want to be the main breadwinner of this family."

For those keeping track at home, that's two references to *Leave It to Beaver*, a popular television series that went off the air in 1963, *people*! Let it go.

To me, the main difference in approach seems to be about transitioning from thinking about breadwinning in the context of gender toward thinking about yourself as part of a team. The men who are most comfortable with what their partner makes seem to spend less time thinking about what men or women are supposed to do, and tend to concentrate on what the best option for their specific partnership is.

For instance, I talked to some stay-at-home dads. Or, in the case of John Rick, stay-at-home-dog-dads. In 2016, both John Rick and his wife, Brij, were commuting three hours round-trip every day into the city of Seattle. After the presidential election that year, they looked at each other and said, "Fuck it." They sold their house for a 65 percent profit and bought a couple of acres out in the woods, off the grid.

When I say off the grid, I mean like way, way off the grid. Their dogs play and run by the lake. Their water comes from a well. There's always plumbing work. Someone's got to trim the orchard. Last summer, they raked 3,000 pounds of pine needles.

"In the winter it really is four to eight hours a day of just shoveling snow, carrying firewood, doing dishes, making food," John Rick says. "Town's a half hour away, so going to get groceries is a two- to three-hour trip. And frankly, sometimes, depending on the road, I have to rig a sled to the back of my snowmobile and sled the groceries three or four miles from the house."

The nearest town has a population of 2,000 in the winter and 10,000 during summer. John Rick's career is fairly specialized, dealing with data security, and he knew ahead of time he wouldn't be able to find work in that industry (besides the occasional freelance telecommuting gig). So he teaches skiing down the hill (he skis to get there) and does odd jobs for friends. Last year he made about $6,000.

They live, essentially, on Brij's salary. She runs communications for a government entity in their area and makes close to six figures.

"Brij has the financial opportunity here to really succeed," John Rick says. "I have no problem taking care of the house and supporting our partnership. . . . I mean, unless I go back to school and get a master's or a JD, I'm never going to make as much as her. I'm not saying I don't want to work, because I do. I'm just saying, at current, both of us working means we can't live where we want to live."

Again, note that John Rick is more concentrated on the partnership than his role. He's pretty comfortable with each person contributing differently based on what they can offer. For instance, he's pretty "manly" in other, more traditional ways. A lot of his day involves snowmobiling or wielding an ax. But Brij chops down the trees.

"Brij—because she used to be a park ranger—has the special certification so she's licensed to run chain saws," John Rick says. "She does all our saw work. I literally stand back and watch her in her pink hard hat and armored chaps bringing down thirty- to forty-foot trees while I'm cheering her on. And I don't touch the chain saw. It is her chain saw."

John Rick's awareness that there are more ways to provide than financially comes from his father. Or rather, through his father's deficiencies. His father was a highly acclaimed doctor. He would work ten hours a day at the hospital, and then five more at the office, he says.

"And while he was around, I never interacted with my dad," John Rick says. "From an early age, I had an understanding— because my mom would tell me—that it's because Dad supports us. I knew as a kid, but I understood later in life, that being a supporter does not mean being a good partner. It does not mean being a good parent. These are different things."

In other words, there's a pretty huge range of ways one can provide, and money is just one of them. A lot of times, having a kid opens up new ways to provide. Jason, thirty, was a full-time butcher when his wife got pregnant.

"We did the math, and paying for child care would eat up most of my paycheck," Jason says. "Pay someone almost all of my own pay to raise my own child? No way."

So Jason quit his job. He picks up part-time work some nights and weekends. His wife is a public school teacher, which they saw as far more secure and steady. Jason can jump back into his career whenever their kid is old enough for him to go back to work.

"I hate the idea of some person raising my child for me, and I hate the idea even more of me working full-time to *pay* some person to raise my child for me," Jason says. "We will likely only have one child, and you only get each moment once, so I want to make sure I am there for every moment that I can be, every step, every word, every encounter, at least until they are old enough to not want me hanging on their shoulder all the time."

I asked Jason point-blank if he felt like having his wife become the breadwinner affected his manliness.

"I didn't notice my masculinity taking a hit when we decided that I would likely stay at home," he says. "I had thought, pretty much from the start, that while I wasn't financially providing for my child, I was providing it with love. Being a parent has never been, at least to me, about giving your kid all the things it wanted, and paying for all of life's incidentals. It was always more about raising it to be an informed member of this society, knowing how the world really works, and preparing it for all of the ups and downs that might come."

Jason had already always done the household chores. He cooks and cleans, does the laundry and the grocery shopping. He plans to clean up baby puke and change his fair share of poopy diapers.

Doing the household chores in addition to having a job is what's called the Second Shift. The term comes from Arlie Russell Hochschild, a sociologist at the University of California, Berkeley, who wrote a book titled *The Second Shift* in 1989. The basic idea of *The Second Shift* is that your first shift is what you do for money, or how you sell your labor at your job. Then the second one is all the work you do, unpaid, at home.[16]

According to a study by A Woman's Nation, less than 20 percent of men do household work after coming back from their jobs, but half of employed women do. Only a third of men report doing more household work than their partners. Less than a fourth say they do more when it comes to parenting. In Japan, it's particularly brutal, according to a *New York Times* article from February 2019.[17] Women work an average of 49 hours a week at their jobs, and then come home and do an average of 25 hours of household chores. Men do 5 hours.

So I guess the question I'm wondering about is, if your partner makes more than you, will you still expect her to carry the load at home too? You'll note that this is very far from the question of "Are you still manly if she makes more?" For many couples, the person making more will vary as careers do.

Actor Tony Goldwyn is one example of someone who has at times made less than his partner and at times made more. You are likely familiar with Goldwyn. He's an actor who's had starring roles in *Ghost*, *The Last Samurai*, and Shonda Rhimes's popular ABC series *Scandal* as the heartthrob President Fitzgerald Grant. His voice has even been featured in Disney's animated adaptation of *Tarzan*.

"[My wife] Jane and I have always had this sort of like fifty-fifty policy about everything. Fifty-fifty parenting, fifty-fifty financial," Goldwyn says. "And [splitting responsibilities evenly] has not come true. Financially, we're going up and down. What's mine is hers and what's hers is mine. Early on, she made a lot more money than me, and then things shifted as my career evolved."

Even before the #MeToo movement, Goldwyn got involved in issues surrounding women's equality. Since then, he's spoken about his own casting couch sexual harassment and how men can be allies during this time. However, he still finds himself having to intentionally curb his instincts when it comes to money in his marriage.

"Sometimes with money, I'll dictate the way things have to be, in this very old-fashioned male way," Goldwyn admits. "And then I have to constantly check myself. Shut up and listen. What is she saying? Often she is correct or has a point, but I have this in my DNA sometimes, an impulse to sort of claim privilege."

Another area he's had to work on with his wife is a more equitable split of the household duties.

"I'd be doing a movie somewhere, and she'd just handle everything," he says. "But resentments built up over years, and there came a point in our relationship where we had to have a real airing of those resentments that built up because our relationship got into a crisis."

Goldwyn wasn't even aware of the extra work he had been tacitly asking his wife to do. Or at least he wasn't aware until it came to a head.

"So then all this stuff came out, and I was like, 'What, really?' She had this deep anger and resentment about that. It was a real wake-up call for me," he says. "I realized how much I needed to remain conscious of it. We're still not even, but I must say I do pull my weight, and try. It's a constant back-and-forth and negotiation. It's a learning process."

Thirty years into his marriage, Goldwyn is *still* learning how to contribute to his relationship outside of finances, so maybe we can cut ourselves some slack. But that doesn't let everyone off the hook for not searching out other ways to contribute.

"It's about encouraging people to detach from this idea that making the most money means anything beyond just making money," Alptraum says. "Just degendering this idea of making more money and the idea of being a provider. There's also more than one way to provide for your family. Financial provider is just one way."

Men still have easier access to money, so perhaps for the majority of relationships it might still make sense for the man to contribute more financially. "But I think we have to divorce the idea that how much money you make connects to your self-worth, regardless of gender," Alptraum says.

What's *your* value in your relationship? What makes you feel good to contribute, what makes your partner feel good to contribute, and how can you best divvy up what's left over?

"You know I've often said that men's basic trait is to feel needed, and women's basic trait is to feel cherished," Dr. Helen Fisher says.

Just keep in mind there's more than one way to be needed. There's more than one way to feel cherished.

SHOULD WE SHARE A BANK ACCOUNT?

Almost one out of five people under 37 don't know how much their partner makes. And 28 percent of the same age group (23–37) keep their finances separate from a partner. This is far more prevalent than it was for previous generations; the same Bank of America report says that only 11 percent of Gen Xers and 13 percent of baby boomers have separate finances. Part of the reason is that younger generations are getting married later. In 1960, the median age for a first marriage was 20 years for women and 22 years for men. Now it's almost 28 for women and almost 30 for men.[18]

By the time you're cresting thirty, you've already got your own bank account and credit score and probably student loan payments and whatnot. Merging those is a chore. Of course, there's also the idea of financial feminism I mentioned earlier in the chapter.

"My mom really instilled in us the sense of having to be self-sufficient, to not rely on somebody else for our financial needs," Brij says. She also pointed out that this message intensified after her parents got divorced. "I almost think it's a little bit of intergenerational trauma that gets passed down between women in this country, around being able to have that self-sufficiency and to set yourself up so you don't have to be only beholden to another person."

Take Davos and Erika, for example. Erika came from a history of money fraud in her family, so it was very important to her to keep their finances totally separate. "Money now is a fairly even split," Davos says. "We share rent and health insurance down the middle." It's down to the penny. They even considered that Davos should pay more for the eggs, since he had a bigger appetite than Erika and eats more eggs per week than her. Davos thought this was odd, but he loves Erika, so they make it work. Now he likes to keep things even and separate. It seems fair.

But that's not the question at hand. You want to know if *you* should join accounts with your partner.

I have an easy answer for that!

Just kidding. You're going to have to read some more words and then figure out how to apply them to your own life.

I first started thinking about this question while considering my own personal finances, which I had never combined with another person, but was considering doing in my current relationship. At the time, I was hosting my television show for Univision and interviewing people from all over the country, so on the side, in between camera shots, I started asking people how they handled personal finances with their significant other, and the answers really ran the gamut.

A 2019 article in *New York* magazine's *The Cut* called "When Two Bank Accounts Become One"[19] laid out some pretty interesting new data that confirmed much of what I had been hearing. For one, couples who pool their money are happier in their relationship and less likely to break up.[20] But not only that (because *obviously* happier couples are more likely to pool money), multiple studies also show that the couples were happier *after* joining their accounts, so it's a causal relationship. Couples who pooled all their money in joint accounts were the happiest, those with joint and individual accounts were the next happiest, and couples who kept separate accounts were least happy. (I should note that this held only for couples who had been together for longer than a year. So if you just started dating, maybe keep doing Venmo ping-pong.)

A paper about these studies written by researchers from UCLA, Notre Dame, and University College London suggested a reason for this. They call it "financial togetherness." If your finances are joined, it creates an idea of shared financial goals. You're on the same team, pulling in the same direction.[21]

Let's meet another couple: Sam comes from less money than her husband, David, so she's very careful and mindful of money. At different times in their relationship, each one has made more than the other. They've been together for a long time, so they support each other like a team. All their money goes into one account, which Sam manages to pay the bills. She gives David . . . an allowance. "A what?" I asked when I spoke with David. "An allowance," he told me.

He does not find that at all infantilizing. "We get money, she delegates all of the bills and all that stuff, and then shoots me some money every two weeks," David says. "And I like that, because I'm not the most detail-oriented when it comes to budgeting."

David says some colleagues who know about the arrangement get a kick out of it. But he's beyond feeling any shame about it; this is what works for their relationship.

Priya Malani from Stash Wealth advises all of her clients to merge bank accounts. "Our goal is to get clients to think and work as a team in a relationship. Husband/husband, wife/wife, husband/wife, whatever it is, we're telling them it doesn't matter who makes more," Malani says. "It doesn't matter who has more debt. This is the 'one team, one dream' mentality."

She pointed out a key flaw in the idea that women should have separate accounts as a lifeline: that won't help much in the case of divorce.

"What they don't realize is if you don't have a prenup in place, the law sees you as a team anyway, so you're not protected; you just *think* you're protected," Malani says. "If you run into a situation, all the assets get pooled and divided equally."

Malani does have one tiny caveat to her company's joint-account rule. They recommend having all income directly deposited into one shared account, out of which all bills and spending are split. However, she lets each person keep a separate account with a small stipend. She recommends about two hundred dollars a month. Whatever you spend out of that amount, you don't have to justify to your partner—ever—so you can both lend a small amount to your failure-to-launch family members without a blowout fight. The key is to be on the same page with your financial goals. And there's absolutely no way to do this besides talking to each other. A lot. And candidly.

Couples fight about money more than anything else, according to *Money* magazine. In fact, 70 percent of couples argue more about money than sex, snoring, chores, or what's for dinner.

But how do you avoid just making it another fight?

Dr. Jenn Mann has a few ideas. She's a therapist who has her own VH1 show, *Couples Therapy with Dr. Jenn*, and she hosts a Sirius XM call-in show, *The Dr. Jenn Show*. She most recently published the book *The Relationship Fix*. Mann recommends, instead of waiting until money becomes a problem and bickering about it, set aside consistent scheduled time to talk finances. Writing for *InStyle*, she laid out her ground rules:[22]

Try to keep meetings under twenty minutes, she says. Do them weekly. No TV, phones, or computers. Keep notes. Pick a leader and set an agenda each week. Take turns talking, do not interrupt, and discuss one topic at a time. Move on when both are satisfied. Decisions need to be unanimous. Unresolved issues can be tabled, or you should have a trusted third party who can help mediate. And lastly, don't sneak. According to that *Money* magazine survey, 22 percent of respondents admitted to hiding purchases from their spouses.[23]

The earliest meetings will be the hardest. Once you've been doing it a few years, you'll probably just mention that you found twenty dollars on the sidewalk or something and adjourn.

Some of the big discussions Mann recommends for early meetings include setting a budget and spending limits, establishing bank accounts, picking a tracking system like QuickBooks, choosing your third-party mediator, and being open about your money anxieties.

If this sounds like a hell of a lot of talking about money, it is.

"How many times do you talk about something until you don't have to talk about it anymore?" Kyle Wright says his clients ask him. "I'm like, 'Well, guess what? Never.' You're going to talk about communication in your relationship forever. You're going to talk about money and your relationship forever. So start getting good at it. It's never going to stop."

Conversations about money will become increasingly easier

once you and your partner are on the same page about what the underlying goals are—what you are using the money for and why.

"We can tell within the first meeting if they're not on the same page with their goals," Milani says. "And goals relate directly to values. And if you're not on the same page with your values, where is this relationship going?"

Money *is* survival in our current age, so it makes sense that it's a thorny issue with a lot of emotional baggage. It gets at the core of what we value—and our own value. The men I spoke to had varying ideas about how much, if at all, money impacted their self-worth. It surprised some men to realize they wanted to hark back to the past and have a *Leave It to Beaver* type of life. Others were trying to make their parents proud. And others seemed to have completely moved past that idea.

We're in the midst of a huge generational shift. Not only that, we're in a societal shift. These things take time—ten thousand years of generational expectation won't die overnight. As we navigate these changes, there are two concepts I keep coming back to: One is the need to degender the idea of providing, particularly financially. And two is viewing your partner with a team mentality.

This will become particularly important if you're a parent.

Chapter 5
PARENTING

J im was hiding in the kitchen, secretly eating the tacos while everyone else was in the living room, and then he overheard the toast.

This was a fortieth birthday party for his sister-in-law, who was visiting from Maine.

"The party thinned out and it was just the family left, and everyone gets pretty drunk," Jim remembers. "And the toast she gave was something like, 'The age of women is here! The age of white men is OVER.'"

Jim stopped mid-guilt-bite and had to consider what was happening. Jim, by the way, is a white man.

He thought, "This is weird because you're in my house and I agree with you—but I feel like I'm being put in an impossible position because I'm part of the oppressor class, so I'm part of the problem." Honestly, he told me, "It felt weird and it felt icky!"

He remembers thinking, "But who is going to represent me if there's no white men allowed in power anymore? That doesn't seem fair, either."

Things got really deep for Jim really quickly, right there in his kitchen on his sister-in-law's fortieth birthday. Before he knew it, he was thinking about what manhood is, what it looks like, and how it's created, which then made him think of his son. "And so to get to parenting, I don't even know what it means to teach my son how to be a man, because I don't even know what that is! I do identify as a man, but I don't even know what that means, and is that something I can be proud of?

"We lack coming-of-age rituals for men and, because we don't have them, we go into the world confused about how to be," he says. "We as a society don't provide tools around integrity creation. It's a problem, and I think it could get even worse because men are coming from a place of defensiveness. Like when I heard that speech being given in my house, I'm like: Wait, that's a little scary."

Now that his son is two, Jim has been considering the development of manhood in earnest. There's a time crunch involved now. "And how do you teach something you don't understand yourself?" he asks.

HOW DO I RAISE A SON TO BE A "GOOD MAN" WHEN I DON'T KNOW WHAT THAT IS ANYMORE?

Parenting is tricky, if not nigh impossible, at the best of times. There are approximately 20 zillion parenting blogs you can spend the rest of your child's life reading. Everyone who ends up on a therapist's couch talks about their parents.

Let me disclose here very quickly that I don't have any children, but you don't need to be a parent to realize that the cultural conversation right now is impacting how people are thinking about raising their kids. When a relative of mine's wife, we'll call her Sarah, was expecting their first child, she told me they had just found out it was a girl, and, to be quite honest, she was initially disappointed by that because Sarah had wanted a boy. But, she told me, a friend had recently reminded her, "A girl! Thank God. Who would want to a raise a boy right now?!"

That is a good question! How do you raise a boy right now—in the era of #MeToo, consent, and "Grab 'em by the pussy"? It strikes me as this added layer of confusion—if no one really knows what they're doing right now, how do you make sure to throw the bathwater out, but not the baby? After I spoke with her, I started asking parents in various settings—business meetings, cocktail mixers, exercise dates—what, if anything, has changed about the way people are approaching child rearing in light of the cultural shifts that the #MeToo movement has caused.

I'll discuss raising boys for the majority of this chapter, in part because of my relative's prompt, but also because we often spend a lot of time focusing on how our daughters can be taught to be strong, independent, to protect themselves, and to fight the world they're raised into—which are all important things. But there is much less emphasis on raising "good boys"—whatever that means. People often say it's much easier to raise boys because you don't have to worry about them as much. But maybe we should a little more, so let's dive into that first.

Jim said one thing that has really stuck with me: "I don't know what it means to teach my son how to be a man, because I don't even know what that is."

I asked him to explain.

"So what do you tell your son about what being a man is?" he says. "That phrase—'Be a man'—that feels like it's going out the window now. Or at least it should. So how do you teach that when it's become so murky?"

In other words, what is masculinity?

We probably need to figure out what that is before we can teach it to our children, and while most men are being told that their masculinity is toxic, it would help to figure out what positive parts of masculinity we want to pass along to the next generation.

That's a puzzler for most of you.

"Masculinity has always been a prison to me. I grew up with no real male role models. As I grew older, getting my ass kicked at school taught me that I wasn't adhering to what being a 'man' meant. I started rejecting the concept entirely, but I didn't actually know how to do that." —*Tim, 36*

"I think the concept of masculinity is a very loose term and open to different interpretations for different people, and, as I'm finding out by trying to dive into this topic, is often misunderstood or even conflated with ideas such as dominance and inflexibility. Masculinity, to me, is simply a collection of qualities like strength, dependability, integrity, virility, honor, reason, and bravery. But the funny thing is that none of them are specifically male qualities. So, that's why I say it's a loose concept." —*Stephan Badyna, 34,* A Pod Amongst Men *podcast host*

"Masculinity means almost nothing to me other than a textbook definition of it, which I think is useless in today's world. A woman can be masculine, and man can be feminine. These labels add nothing to defining a person, and should be abandoned. Modern manhood means you are keeping up with the times, and not letting your past mistakes define you. . . . [It's] standing up for what you believe in, and being willing to defend it, having the confidence to not have to be physical to get your point across, and being able to deescalate a situation that might become physical. [It's] realizing that there are people who depend on you, and not taking selfish paths in life that might be destructive or otherwise reckless." —*Jason, 30*

For most of us, our first worldview came from our parents. We learned what a man is from the type of man the men in our lives were. Ideally, you had a great dad and a great relationship and you don't even need to read this chapter! But maybe not.

For instance, take Javier, the thirty-three-year-old Mexican-American from Florida, whose dad showed a lot of tough love because, as Javier sees it, that's how his grandfather raised his dad. "Growing up, he was always frustrated with me whenever I wasn't as good at sports as he expected, or became emotional whenever he was upset with me. Those experiences affected me greatly," Javier says. "I was extremely shy and would cower in front of others. As I got older, I began developing anxiety. I would constantly have panic attacks and would be worried or overthink the smallest things. I was also in a constant state of depression because I was always seeking validation or approval on anything I was doing. I know I don't want to be that kind of father for my son. The one thing I always promised myself was that as a father I'd never get physical with my son—and I don't allow anyone to do so. I've found other methods to be as effective, without having to inflict fear. I also want him to be sure he knows that any punishments or criticisms are with reason. There should always be a lesson taught," Javier tells me.

That probably sounds familiar. We either want our kids to have a similar upbringing as our own, or else we want to make sure to not repeat mistakes of the past.

"I'm going to strive to teach my son that strength comes in many forms, and that traditional roles and expectations do not define who he is as a person," Javier says.

In the past several years, many of you have had to reexamine what manhood is in light of a lot of the discussions from the #MeToo movement, and while you are processing these dynamics, you are simultaneously trying to teach your new sons what masculinity is. It's tricky! The average age of first-time fathers in the United States is rising: it's 30.9 years old now.[1] But having kids in your twenties is still wildly popular, which means it's not like you get to figure out life completely and then make the calm, intentional decision to have children and pass along your collected wisdom to them. You just kind of figure it out as you go.

Dan Doty is rare in that he got a little bit of a head start. He had already been thinking about this kind of thing while holding various jobs. After college, he worked as a wilderness therapy guide for young men, and he taught two years at a public high school in the Bronx while getting his master's before moving into media, specifically outdoors TV shows. Two and a half years ago, he had his first son at the age of thirty-four.

"When he was born, it was like a lightning bolt in my gut that said, 'Okay. All this stuff you know you have to bring to the world? It's now personal,'" he says. "'If you don't do this, if you don't share this with the world, you're literally taking away from your son's future.'"

Doty helped cofound Evryman, an organization that runs weekly groups and retreats in order "to better inspire and improve the lives of men, the communities they participate in, and humanity at large." Evryman has been covered by the *New York Times*, the *Today* show, *Men's Health*, and, oh yeah, ever hear of a little podcast called *The Joe Rogan Experience*? (Dan taught Joe how to hunt.)

"I want my son to be healthy, but I also want to help the world be more healthy for him," Doty says. "So that's where I'm coming from. That's where Evryman came from. That's when it started, when my son was born."

As he parents his son and talks to other men, he's come up with a few ideas on how to raise his boys.

"The first step that needs to happen is that fathers themselves need an opportunity to slow the hell down and to uncover all of the spectrum of their selves," Doty says. "Their vulnerable parts, their emotional lives, all the different parts that men have been culturally excluded from having and feeling. It starts there."

This makes sense to me. If men glean from their fathers what masculinity is, dads should probably be intentionally figuring out how they want to model it. For plenty of men, that can involve *feelings*.

"In order to deal with other people's emotions—such as your kids in all of their states—if they are expressing emotions that you yourself are not capable of feeling, and not comfortable feeling, you're screwed," he says. "All of the 'don't cry, toughen up'—there's a lot of ways to look at it, but one of the more simple and sad ways is that guys just don't have that capacity. They're not capable of softening, so of course they tell their kids not to do it. It makes them uncomfortable."

There's an idea that it's unmanly to admit you have feelings. I'll get into this in the friendship chapter, but if you were raised like that, it's going to take a conscious effort to tap into parts of yourself you want your children to be able to healthily tap into later in their lives. For men, says Doty, this can involve having to work through your own shit, and it can come up before you're necessarily ready to go through that.

But trust, this is not just a challenge for men. Let me give you a tangible example of how one woman pushed through her discomfort. (We really are all on the same team here!)

Lea Aella is a motivational speaker as well as a sexual assault survivor. After splitting up with her husband, she found herself trying to figure out how to raise a son in the wake of her own trauma.

"I just basically abandoned every traditional construct there is," she says. "And one of those areas was realizing how much shame my parents had instilled in me around sex. It really left me unprepared to navigate the world of expressing consent and understanding my boundaries and connecting intimately when I was an adult."

Her son is six now, and she's trying to start incorporating ideas about sex into her conversations with him. She doesn't want to leave it up to the school system. However, she's an only child, so young boys are like aliens to her, she told me, and given her internalized shame in talking about sex, it's uncomfortable for her to talk about. So, she bought a book called *It's Not the Stork!*, which uses a cartoon bird and bee to walk through the conversation in age-appropriate terms.[2]

"Let me tell you, when I got to the page about actual sex, I was faced with reading the names of the body parts, which I've always had trouble doing," she says. "I'm trying to force these words like 'gonads' and 'semen' through, and I'm pushing through it, and I'm saying these things and I'm fighting back laughter."

But when she looked at her children (she also has a ten-year-old stepdaughter and fifteen-year-old stepson), they were looking back at her with genuine curiosity. They started asking earnest questions without shame.

"And it dawns on me that they have not yet had any shame layered onto them about this subject, and that this was a critical juncture I had them at where I could influence how they think about that," she says. "If I had acted shameful and giggly, they might have been like, 'Why is that funny?' and I don't know how I would have explained it."

Her real parenting moment came when describing the actual mechanics of sex. She was reading from the book about how, when a man and a woman come so close together, he goes inside her, and all the while she was silently screaming in her head. Her son, however, was soaking it up. "He made me read that part two more times to understand, and then he started [repeating it] back [to me] so he could understand," she remembers.

"He said, 'Okay, Mommy. So when a boy becomes a man and he loves the woman, he gives her a baby.' And I said, 'Yes, that is one way that happens.' And he goes, 'Okay. So when I turn into a man, I'm going to give you a baby.'"

Aella continues, "And I'm like, 'Oh my God! Mayday! Please don't ever say that to your father!'"

She laughs now when she tells the story, especially because she feels like she successfully conveyed that love can lead to a child and that he understood it.

"It was so beautiful and sweet and innocent," she says. "And then I had to kind of break his little heart." She will not, in fact, be having a child with her son.

Still, she's proud of pushing through her own hang-ups about sex and breaking patterns that were passed down to her from previous generations. Her parents used to run away—literally pretend something was on the stove and vacate the room—when she asked them about sex as a young woman. Or they would cover her eyes during risqué scenes on TV.

"To have that level of integrity and disclosure and authenticity in talking about that, it was like I wasn't just dumbing the world down for him," she says. "And for him to have that insight so early, it felt really refreshing that I could create a safe place for him to ask those questions."

When he was three, he asked Lea if it's ever okay to touch himself. She knew what he meant, because he used a kid term for penis.

"I was just so happy that he asked *me* this question before asking my mom [his grandmother], who would be like, 'We don't talk about that' or 'No, it's not okay' or something," she says. "I knelt down and I said, 'Oh sweetie, of course it is okay to touch yourself. Your body belongs to you and that's totally fine. But the one thing I want to say is that there's a right time to do that.' I gave him this trick to remember, 'Touch our privates in private, not in public.'"

She ran him through scenarios to make sure he understood. Like, can he touch himself when he's alone in his bedroom? Yes, of course. What about at Nana's dinner table? Nope, that's public. Again, he was three.

"It feels like that's what parenting is about. It's about deciding the kind of global community member you want to raise," she says. "And awareness of shame around sex is critical I think in this day and age—not even removing it. [I mean] not putting it on to begin with."

This hints at the second lesson Doty has learned: that we need to meet boys where they're at. Instead of imposing shame and a set of beliefs about sex on her son, Aella was meeting him on his level and letting him develop his own understanding of it, as gently but openly as possible.

"We need to teach our boys to be themselves," Dan Doty says. "Our job is to make space to have our boys be themselves and to encourage that and to love them for it."

He thinks boys need examples for guidance and space to develop. They probably do not need a set of rigid expectations placed on them.

"We know this by now! We know this is human. We know that when your true nature is stifled or told it's wrong or told to be different . . ." Doty trails off, but you can fill in the rest. "I think with boys right now it's so poignant."

Your son might be gay. Your son might like talking about his emotions more than you're comfortable with. Or, your son might root for the Yankees. None of that lessens the need to love and listen to him. A better way to approach this might be to hear what your kids have to teach you about the human condition, rather than you transferring a set of beliefs onto them.

"Parents have to start listening to their children more," says Niobe Way, Ph.D., a professor of developmental psychology at New York University and the author of *Deep Secrets: Boys' Friendships and the Crisis of Connection.* Dr. Way is well-known in her field for her research over the last thirty years on boys and childhood development. "So less than what do parents have to teach their children, I would flip it into what do children have to teach parents about what we need? Reminding us! Reminding us of what we as humans want and what drives us."

Here's an example of that.

"My son likes to wear dresses," Jim says. "I think probably because he has an older sister." It might be a phase. It might not. Who knows.

"It doesn't bother me now, but I think it did at first," Jim admits.

"My social conditioning muscle made it bother me, and then I thought, *Well, why should it bother me? That's ridiculous.*"

Sometimes boys wear dresses, and sometimes I wear pants. Watching his son dress up helped Jim internalize that. It bugged him at first, until he could hold that emotional reaction to the light and consciously work through it. Listening to his son is definitely part of how he got there.

A twenty-six-year-long study found that if parental values are imparted in a loving way, children will eventually adopt their parents' beliefs, even if they rebel against them temporarily while trying to carve out their own identities.[3] From that we can gather that if you really want your kid to absorb your beliefs, a better long-term plan is to communicate with compassion. According to Dr. Niobe Way's research, as boys develop into young men they tend to lose "emotional acuity and insight," meaning after their mid-teen years, men are less encouraged by society to reflect on, understand, and articulate what they're feeling. And, Dr. Way points out, if they maintain emotional acuity past their mid-teens, it's because someone with a significant role in their life as an adolescent encouraged them to process and talk openly about their emotions.

"In their adolescence or somehow in the early years they had someone who was really nurturing those capacities," Dr. Way says.

According to her research, it's often a mother, but can also be a grandparent or an older sibling. It could even be you.

"All children, regardless of gender identity, come with an extraordinary capacity for relationships and for emotional attunement and for reading each other's feelings," she says.

Right now, you might be asking yourself, "But what does that look like?" Great, because that's exactly what I asked Dan Doty.

Doty's oldest son, Duke, at two and a half, is, as Doty describes him, "a very physically hesitant, verbally forward child." Very early on, Dan taught him the names of some basic emotions: "sad, angry, ashamed, joyful," and so on.

"If Duke's going through a little tantrum, we'll just slow down," Dan says. "I'll get down on his level and we'll take a few breaths.

We have a sort of a mindfulness breath practice, just like take a deep breath and breathe in."

I took this to mean Dan literally crouches down to the same physical and height level as his toddler, and then after they breathe, Dan will ask Duke what he's feeling.

"He'll say, 'I'm feeling sad and angry,'" or whatever, Doty says. "And then I'll just affirm that. I'll be like, 'Yeah I can see that. And it's okay to be sad and angry,' and we'll just sit there for a minute." Usually it takes Duke twenty seconds or so before he's hugging Dan and smiling, and then they move on.

"He feels his feelings and then he works through it, and this natural, simple process of human emotion [is something] we all have," Doty says.

Honestly, I could probably use someone to do that with me when I get overwhelmed.

OKAY, BUT HOW DO I TEACH SOMEONE ELSE CONSENT?

Imagine yourself as Brett Kavanaugh's father. Across the country, your son's name is synonymous with sexual assault and male privilege. For years to come, a picture of his open yelling mouth will be the visual of not trusting or valuing women.

"If my son grew up to be a Kavanaugh it would feel like the biggest failing as a parent," Jim says. "That's the nightmare scenario."

If you feel similarly, perhaps the first step is to ask yourself why you *don't* want that.

"You hear parents are worried about their sons," says Deborah J. Cohan, Ph.D. "But are you worrying about them being good men and doing the right thing and not doing something wrong? Or"— she pauses—"are you worried about them getting caught?"

Dr. Cohan is a professor of sociology at the University of South Carolina–Beaufort and the author of *Welcome to Wherever We Are: A Memoir of Family, Caregiving, and Redemption*. She began her career researching children who had witnessed family violence, and she has since shifted over to studying those who perpetrate violence in the home. We talked a lot about her past work with violent offenders as she aimed to help them unlearn their patterned behavior.

It was interesting to glean her observations about what nonviolent folks can learn from those who have perpetrated violence. One of her main priorities, she told me, was to teach offenders to take personal responsibility. An important lesson for us all.

And so, let's start with this question: How do you teach consent? According to the experts I spoke with, it's actually a question of teaching empathy.

"Consent is very black-and-white," Haylin Belay, a sexuality consultant and educator in New York City who works primarily with youth, says. As we talked about in the sex chapter, our problem is that when we think of consent in black-and-white terms or legal and not legal, there's a lot that we're missing. "It's just not really a useful framework for talking about sexual activity," says Belay.

There needs to be a word that describes a positive sexual encounter we should model, and "consent" just doesn't really do that because it carries the implication of just covering your bases, says Belay. The closest word that she has come up with is "empathy."

"When I'm talking to a group of young people, I'm not trying to talk to them about the legal boundaries of what they can and can't do without getting in trouble," she says. "I want to talk to them about how can you be empathetic in your relationships with other people in such a way that neither of you leave any interactions—sexual or otherwise—feeling like the other person has taken advantage of, humiliated, or degraded you in some way."

Great, but what does that look like? It turns out, it shows up in different ways at different ages. Dan Doty's wife, for instance, started talking to their son when he was barely a toddler about listening to others when he touches their bodies.

"For example, she's breastfeeding our younger one and so her body gets over-touched already. She's very sensitive to extra touch on top of the baby," Doty says. His two-year-old son Duke "will come up and jump on her without asking, and she'll say 'Duke, this is Mama's body and she's not wanting touch this way right now.'"

When she says she doesn't want to be touched, Duke fully compre-
hends that he needs to stop—full stop.

Belay says these conversations about bodily autonomy, respect-
ing personal boundaries, and caring about how your behaviors make
another person feel should be a common, steady drip throughout
childhood so that the kid feels comfortable coming up and asking
questions about them when they're confused.

So, what does it even mean to teach a profound concept like
empathy to a kindergartner? Belay suggests introducing it to them
at a level they can comprehend, like saying, "Ask first before you
go into someone's bag." Or "Don't hug someone unless you ask
first."

Letting kids know they have autonomy over their own bodies works, too, says Belay. That may look like asking if they want
a good-bye hug. If not, maybe then you settle for a good-bye high
five or a good-bye wave—whatever they feel comfortable with at
the time. This helps embed the idea that they get to choose how
and when they are touched, and that others deserve the same respect.[4]

However, when kids are older than elementary school age, it
can get more complex.

"Middle schoolers are tapped into the social reward system,"
Belay says. "A lot of the things people say and do between the ages
of nine and fourteen are less about their genuine core beliefs and
more about parroting things they've heard and seeing what the
reaction is—that 'edgy' humor or behavior usually isn't reflective
of their actual beliefs or values. So, over time, that 'bad behavior'
crystallizes. For example, some people realize they will be socially
rewarded for callousness or bigotry and then it becomes much
harder to convince them that practicing empathy is worth risking
that social reward."

Belay recounts a workshop she gave to seventh graders at an
all-boys school recently, where they discussed the difference between being a "real man" and a "good man." The kids, Belay says,
identified that these concepts can sometimes be opposites. One of

the students who had been the most challenging and disruptive expressed that he felt like being a "real man" meant goofing off to make his friends laugh and not caring what the teachers thought, but being a "good man" would mean upholding his responsibilities and being respectful to his teacher. He said that sometimes he didn't really want to goof off, but he felt like he had to in order to stay in good standing with his friends.

"The challenge for parents and early childhood educators is, how can we lay a strong foundation so that by the time adolescence rolls around, young boys are more able to withstand the darker sides of peer pressure? And how can we communally raise better sons so that the things that young boys feel like they have to do to be 'cool' aren't things that harm others or themselves?" says Belay. "Middle school is a key time for this."

Because by high school? "High school's too late to start teaching consent to kids," she says.

Whenever she leads exercises with high schoolers, and she explains asking for verbal consent before sex with a partner, she often gets this eyebrow-raising reply: "But if I ask . . . she might say no." As Belay tells me this, she looks at me, alarmed. Like, by the time she gets these kids in high school, they don't want to ask their partners if they want to have sex because they're afraid they'd actually have to listen to them and . . . not have sex. Meaning, they'd rather just not ask and get to have sex with someone even if that person didn't really want to have sex with them in the first place. Belay is always aware that, at that point, this student (and she says there have been many students like this) is already having sex before he's learned how to view his partner's wishes as valid.

Remember when Jim was questioning what "being a man" actually was? "There used to be a phrase like 'act like a man' or 'be a man,' and that meant something," Jim says. "But it feels like something that I would be uncomfortable teaching and I wouldn't even know how to teach it."

For instance, one marker of traditional masculinity that stands out for Jim as supposedly positive is the idea of men as defenders and guardians.

"It's like, are you supposed to be a protector?" Jim muses aloud. "I don't know, because a lot of that stuff that felt noble—like being a good man was a noble thing and now even just putting things in those terms feels completely antiquated and even sexist."

I think this is actually a great point. Where does chivalry play into our modern world? Answers from experts in this space, like renowned researcher and psychologist Peter Glick at Lawrence University, may surprise you. Glick's research focuses on biases, stereotyping, and how to overcome them. He's presented twice at Harvard Business School's conference on gender and work, and he says chivalry is *out*.

"One thing you want to be careful of is teaching boys to be chivalrous," Glick told the *New York Times* in 2018. "We need to stop socializing boys to see women as needing protection."[5]

Glick used the examples of opening doors for others or giving up your seat. Those are kind acts! But instead of doing them for only women, which can help develop the idea that women are fragile or less competent, what if we committed acts of kindness for everyone since it's just the right thing to do? According to Glick, this flips the script of men taking charge while women remain passive, and instead turns it into an exercise in empathy. The former can also be thought of as "benevolent sexism"[6]—a term Glick helped develop and one that I think is quite interesting. Whereas "hostile sexism" is just straight-up misogyny, or the outright hatred of women, benevolent sexism is cloaked in old-timey notions of being a chivalrous gentleman. On the surface, this may appeal to many, like "Listen, I know women don't *need* me to open the door. But I do it because I'm a good guy!" But Glick's research has found that this actually harms women in many ways—and I'm not just talking about reinforcing the idea that women aren't capable of physically protecting themselves. There are more insidious and harder-to-identify implications as well.

For example, as Glick presented at Harvard Business School's Gender & Work symposium in 2013, benevolent sexism can have a detrimental impact on women professionally. Glick suggests that by thinking women need protection, male counterparts may insulate them from more difficult assignments and critical feedback. It can also drain women's personal ambition, says Glick.

So, do we stop teaching our boys chivalry? That might be going too far for a lot us who are attached to more traditional views of protecting and providing. Obviously many of us don't see it like that. I know one woman on Twitter who would tell Glick to go shove his benevolent sexism you-know-where. She tweeted in 2019:

> @Steffi_Cole
>
> It's sad to me that we live in a world where a lot of men refrain from complimenting or being friendly to women because they fear that this will be perceived as sexual harassment.[7]

The responses turned predictably Twitter-rude, but you get the point. Her desire to keep intact more old-school traditions is shared by others all over the country.

"My personal belief, and the way I was raised, is that a man is supposed to be a protector," Charles Edwards says. Edwards is a thirty-three-year-old videographer living in Connecticut. He was raised in an inner-city environment with not a lot of money. He had to grow up pretty quickly, he tells me. Now he's raising two kids in a very different environment than what he grew up in. The kids are growing up wanting for nothing, but he's still preaching some of his lessons from childhood to them. "You're supposed to be a provider, and you're supposed to be that manly figure of your household. But I don't believe that your woman or your partner, whoever it may be, shouldn't be able to do the same."

Edwards has had to think about these things quickly, without being eased into it by watching a son go from newborn to toddler. His partner has two children from a previous relationship, and he's helping raise them. Edwards views his approach as an old-school and new-wave mash-up. He still wants to protect his family, but tries to be aware that they protect him in certain ways, too.

"To me, those are just basic values of the core of being a man. You protect your family, you provide for your family," he says. "But I don't believe you do that by devaluing your woman or what your partner brings to the table and has to offer."

Regardless of your views on chivalry, being more mindful about what you are bringing to the table in terms of your assumptions about masculinity, how comfortable you are expressing your feelings, and being vulnerable will clearly make a big difference when it comes to raising a good man. Plus, teaching your son empathy *now* will be a gift to his partners in the future—and you know he'll thank you for that.

HOW DO I RAISE MY DAUGHTER TO BE A "GOOD WOMAN" WHEN I'M NOT A WOMAN?

How do you raise a girl? Figuring out how to parent a boy is one thing. You were a boy once! So you know the basic outline. But a girl?

As a society, we say raising boys is easy and it's girls who are difficult. Ed, a twenty-nine-year-old technical writer, remembers something his dad said once. "He told me a story about how because my sister [a girl] was their first kid, he was just kind of confused through that whole process," Ed says. "And then at one point after they had me [a boy], my mom came to my dad and was like, 'You have to do the boy, because I don't know how to raise boys.' He said he related to her in the sense that he didn't know how to interact with girls or raise girls."

So what's the difference between boys and girls? Not a whole lot, it turns out.

"As parents, I think we still somehow start from that gender-difference place. We still think that inherently boys are blankety-blank and inherently girls are blankety-blank," Dr. Niobe Way says. "And that's just so damaging. I'm not saying there's no gender differences, but every researcher will say there's much more variety among boys than differences between girls and boys."

To help illustrate her point, Dr. Way used the following example: Men generally have better spatial awareness than women. Is that because of a genetic difference? No. It's because we play catch with boys, play video games with boys, and ride go-karts with boys far more than we do with girls. These sorts of inbuilt gender differences in how we raise children affect how they develop.

"What kills me is how things have gotten even more differentiated for boys and girls," Dr. Lise Eliot, professor of neuroscience at Chicago Medical School, says. "I use the example of school choir. In some communities, it's hard to get boys to sign up to sing. Across all cultures, singing is not a gender-specific thing, but some boys in the United States won't take a singing class or sign up for choir."

Ditto for art classes. As small children, a lot of us loved finger-painting, but getting an elementary-school-aged boy to take an art class? It can be pretty difficult. "Art has become a girl thing," Dr. Eliot says.

To remedy this issue, one fairly easy solution she suggested was to have boys and girls play together as much as possible.

"We need to find more opportunities to prevent the gender segregation that emerges way too young in my opinion," she says. "If a boy and girl play together, don't tease them about getting married and being boyfriend and girlfriend. That just sexualizes them and makes them aware of gender."

Another easy solution is to swap chores. Have your boys do the laundry and make dinner. Ask your girls to mow the lawn. Moreover, what might be most helpful is to *model* these behaviors. Your children learn from you by osmosis.

Many households expect the mother to do the invisible managerial work of running a household. She's in charge of informing the father when they need new sriracha sauce and to pick it up at the store. There's a planning level and then there's the physical action level. Both take time and effort. Picking up some of that invisible work will help indicate to your daughter how to more intentionally split domestic workloads. Parenting and running a household isn't something that's only a woman's job.

Setting a good example in the home sphere is one area of which to be mindful when parenting. But another area that gets parents worked up is daughters and sexuality.

"I think that your kids having sex is really complicated and confusing, and I'll probably have to overcome some prejudice," Jim says. "Like it'll probably bother me more when I learn about my daughter having sex than when my son starts having sex, and I know that that's completely fucked up."

That *is* fucked up. But, if anything, I appreciated Jim's honesty and self-awareness, and his opinion is certainly not a minority opinion based on the responses I've received from men I've interviewed over the years.

Clive is fifty-four and has three daughters in their early twenties.

"I think my daughters are generally quite strong, but I think they can mistake their own sense of empowerment without recognizing the deep-seated entrenched power dynamics beneath the surface, so they may be participating in unempowered dynamics without realizing it," he says. "Particularly in the pornified world where women's sexuality is still often subservient to men's power."

His argument is that they may feel good about themselves by dressing sexy, but aren't they just inadvertently playing into what men want them to do anyway?

"They might feel empowered—like, for example, dressing in a sexually provocative way. I'm like, *Is that an instance of empowerment? Or is that self-sexual objectification?*" he says. "Is it a beautiful liberation or is it fulfilling an inherent expectation?"

This is peak dad. I couldn't help but laugh. My general rule for men: don't ever worry about what a woman is wearing. You wouldn't do it for men.

But let's back up briefly.

You should want your daughter to have a fulfilling sex life, even if the idea gives you the heebie-jeebies. But that also means you can't shame her about sexuality. It means you can't make her think men are dangerous. It means you can't tell her that boys want only one thing.

"Historically women are taught to fear," Lux Alptraum says. "Women are taught to fear men—but in a way that's disempowering, and I think that fathers often play a really, really big part in that."

Alptraum, the author of *Faking It: The Lies Women Tell About Sex—and the Truths They Reveal,* also notes the difference between a "supportive dad" and a "patriarchal dad." A patriarchal dad crows about beating up the men who hurt his daughter and has an "8 Rules for Dating My Daughter" meme posted on his Facebook feed.

"That actually is harmful," Alptraum says. "You should of course be protective of your daughter, and you should of course let her know that if someone does something harmful to her that you will believe her, you will stand by her, and you will provide the support that she needs and wants."

But that's a far cry from telling your daughter that all men are shit.

"Making your daughter live in fear does not prepare her to make healthy choices," Alptraum says. "Whereas raising her to feel ownership of her body and awareness that there are people who are harmful [does]. And awareness of what consent looks like. And also awareness that if she is harmed, that does not tarnish her or somehow make her less than."

To be honest, all of this advice—helping your child recognize her inherent value and empowering her to make healthy decisions for herself without teaching her to fear the world around her—works for your sons, too, and for your nonbinary children. We were raised to be concerned with the good qualities in "men" and "women" and passing them on to our sons and daughters, but would we benefit if we challenged these traditional stereotypes and biases, degendered our parenting approach, and taught our children to become good human beings—rather than good men or good women?

I liked how Lea Aella phrased it: "Decide the kind of global community member you want to raise." And then all you have to do is model that and communicate it compassionately for several decades straight.

Of course, that's much easier said than done, but you could use the practice with your kids because your friends really need your help, too—and that is precisely why I'm diving into that subject next.

Chapter 6
FRIENDS

J im's got a friend named Paul, a multimillion-
aire who works in real estate.

"I love this guy," Jim says. "He's one of those
sort of aggro, hypercompetitive guys. He'll text
me and be like, 'Get on the bike, you fat fuck!!' and
I laugh because it's kind of amusing. He's a pre-
school dad friend and it's like . . . he's so different
than my super-woke dad friends. And it's sort of
refreshing, but he's ridiculous and has old-world
views towards men and women."

Jim says he finds himself deleting his text message chain with Paul so there's no evidence of their
inappropriate texts in case Jim's wife reads his
phone. Recently, both families went out to Sunday
dinner to a Mediterranean restaurant. All four kids
were there, and the two wives started talking to
each other.

"Under the table, Paul showed me a half-naked
photo of a woman with no context," Jim remembers. "I just remember thinking it was wildly

inappropriate. Like, 'Why are you showing me that right now?!'"

Jim couldn't figure out if it was just internet porn or someone Paul was sleeping with. Paul likes to joke about his "next wife," sometimes right in front of his current wife. "It feels like what he's always trying to do is to get other married men on his team . . . it's like a spiritual war between like men and women," Jim explains.

"I didn't shut it down because I didn't have the courage," he continues. "Part of you wants to be part of the group. But not saying something haunts me. But if you do call them out, you're afraid that they'll say, 'Oh, Jim's not cool!' And frankly I'm ashamed of that."

LOCKER ROOM TALK

The thing is, people have been talking like this—in a kind of disrespectful way disguised as playful—for probably as long as there have been people. So, what feels different now? Why am I all of a sudden getting a rash of DMs from men on social media about how—if at all—they're supposed to call their guy friends out for this kind of shitty talk and behavior?

"Guys are more scared now," Jim says. "One minute it was okay to objectify women and then literally overnight it's no longer okay."

What changed?

The #MeToo movement, sure—but, honestly, it feels like Donald Trump's "grab 'em by the pussy" line really transformed this conversation first. In case you've been in a coma for the past few years, during the 2016 presidential election, a clip from *Access Hollywood*[1] leaked that caught Donald Trump bragging about touching women without their permission.

"I'm automatically attracted to beautiful—I just start kissing them. It's like a magnet. Just kiss. I don't even wait," Trump said. "When you're a star, they let you do it. You can do anything. Grab 'em by the pussy. You can do anything."

When Anderson Cooper asked then-candidate Trump about his comments in a debate, Trump said, "I don't think you understood what was—this was locker room talk. I'm not proud of it. I apologize to my family. I apologize to the American people. Certainly, I'm not proud of it. But this is locker room talk."[2]

Spoiler alert: Trump went on to become president of the United States of America.

So, what's locker room talk? Well, not to be too on the nose about it, but you might find it interesting that if you merely look up "locker room" (not "locker room talk") on Merriam-Webster .com,[3] the first definition is "of, relating to, or suitable for use in a locker room, especially: of a coarse or sexual nature." Only the second definition explains that a locker room is actually a place to change clothes.

When I'm in a locker room, I'm usually talking about my workout or recapping my day, but I understand the metaphor: it's generally a single-gendered space where you could ostensibly be more free to speak about other genders in a negative or disparaging way without judgment. Still, this isn't really about me, because I can't think of an instance in popular culture when "locker room talk" has applied to women.

So, the more interesting question is maybe *why* does locker room talk exist for men? Why do some men feel the need to discuss things without women around, or say things they wouldn't in public? As it turns out, this might have something to do with how a lot of male friendships are built.

"From my lens, friendships between males has often been centered around an external force. We are doing this activity together. We're either on a sports team, we're in college together—we have this external thing outside of us around which we connect," Dan Doty says. "What happens there is that men build identities based on this external thing, and when that external thing no longer is strong or it shifts or it's not the same anymore, then [we] are left kind of hanging. There's not that practice to build relationships based on [simply] being. Like, here's me. Here's who I am underneath these other things. Here's me underneath the things I like to do." Meaning, male friendships and conversations might not be built around deep conversations and emotional intimacy, so locker room talk stands in for male bonding.

Research shows men often establish friendships based on inclusion of an "in-group" at the expense of an "out-group." Essentially, you create a "them" to better define the "us." This makes a lot of sense, to be honest. We relate more to people who are like us. Stanford neuroscientist David Eagleman did a study where he showed participants images of others in pain. Under fMRIs, this activated people's brains in the areas they would feel their own pain. But it wasn't one-for-one. The extent could be altered depending on if they identified with the person in pain, in this case, based on shared religion.[4] So we care more, even on a physical level, for those we view as part of our group.

How does this relate back to men and women? Think about it. You've almost definitely been in situations where—maybe not in a locker room, and maybe not in a frat house, but somewhere—men made women the out-group in order to build camaraderie. This is due to a primal need. We all want to belong, to fit in somewhere. The American Psychological Association published a study that found that "the need to belong is a powerful, fundamental, and extremely pervasive motivation"—so much so that a lack of attachments can be brutally detrimental, even to your physical health.[5]

Along the same line, a study by Betsy Paluck, a professor of psychology and public affairs at Princeton University, found that schoolchildren base their views of bullying on what other classmates think.[6] Basically, if all of our friends are saying bullying is fine, we're less likely to push against that even in our own lives— and that's true of pretty much any issue, including joking about grabbing vaginas.

Locker room talk is an attempt to bond by creating a shared

out-group. However, it's important to differentiate here. The desire to bond and connect with others is healthy and universal, but the results to the out-group can be damaging.

"Women can be the out-group as long as we somehow think that there's a fundamental difference between men and women," Dr. Niobe Way says. "That's the harm of all our gender difference, racial difference, class difference—it's created a world where we truly think that men and women are fundamentally different." As you may remember, Dr. Way is a psych professor at NYU who has studied the development of young boys for the last thirty years. She is also the former president of the Society for Research on Adolescence (SRA) and codirector of the Center for Research on Culture, Development, and Education at NYU. Her research on male adolescent development is often cited by others in the space, so much so that when I sent her pre-interview questions for our interview, she told me she's so used to talking to press, she didn't need them. She continues, "And so that creates an enormous problem, because then what happens is that we're all trying to get on top. We live in a hierarchy, and as long as we say that those on the bottom are fundamentally different from those of us on the top, or vice versa, it generates dehumanization."

Think of Brett Kavanaugh again, and think of the women who accused him of sexual assault. Dr. Christine Blasey Ford says he restrained her and tried to take off her clothes, while he and another friend laughed. Deborah Ramirez says he put his penis in her face in front of a group of people, while laughing. Kavanaugh claims he was still a virgin at the time. That may be true! He didn't have sex with either of the women. What he is accused of doing, though, is laughing (and bonding) with other drunk males while female bodies became the expendable casualties.

Spoiler alert: Brett Kavanaugh is now a Supreme Court justice.

Hopefully, you haven't been in a situation like the above. But there are more subtle forms of this situation—for example, Jim's friend, who likes to bond with him by putting other women down (including his wife) and casually sharing naked photos of other women. If we give Jim's friend the benefit of the doubt, it's not that he's an asshole. It's probably just that he's trying to connect with Jim in the only way he knows how.

WAIT, SO WHAT'S THE DIFFERENCE BETWEEN "LOCKER ROOM TALK" AND SEX TALK?

I've found that a lot of men are genuinely confused about what they're allowed to say and talk to each other about—Jim included. Like, can you still talk about sex stuff with your guy friends, or is that "locker room talk"?

"I feel more of an onus to process my own complicity in this stuff, but the problem is it's really scary because there's also a lot of finger-pointing going on, and I think that we're sort of in fight-or-flight mode," Jim says of men like himself who are wanting to better themselves—but also not wanting to get dragged through the mud.

I can empathize here.

Let's say something weird happened during your last hookup—there was a baby carriage in the bedroom and she never mentioned it. Or she nicknamed your penis right away. Or you had never seen nipples like hers before. Can you still bring that up to friends after?

"I definitely talk to my friends about sexual experiences. I don't think there's anything wrong with it," Stephan Badyna says. Stephan is a thirty-four-year-old husband, stepdad, and contractor in New Jersey who just launched a new podcast called *A Pod Amongst Men* to create a safe space for his guy friends as they navigate a world filled with "punks, pricks, cowards, cornballs, douchebags, dickheads, fakers, and fuckbois." (His words—not mine.)

"Listen," he says. "Men and women both talk to their friends about those things. When does it become locker room talk? I think 'locker room talk' is mainly in reference to the cruder and more braggadocious side of that, when you talk about your experiences as conquests."

It's one thing to recount your sexual experiences with a friend, but once you start speaking about your experience as a conquest, you're dehumanizing the person you've just been intimate with.

And there does seem to be a crucial difference in motivation. Do you want to brag? Or are you genuinely looking for advice? Perhaps what you should consider is if you're making women—or any particular woman—part of the out-group in an effort to bond with your male friends.

"Generally, I find that the more experienced a man is, the more caring and concerned he is about the feelings he has for a woman, or his partner (or whatever), or the impression he offers of her in the way he speaks," Rich says. "I often feel inclined to just take it easy on myself and my guy friends, while also pressing the perspective with them and in my own mind that these are people we're talking about—not dolls, props, or otherwise."

The follow-up question there is why *shouldn't* you talk about women like they're props? If it's helping you bond with other men and it's just a joke anyway, what's the harm to her? A woman you hooked up with has weird nipples! Surely, it's not a crime to let some of your buddies know? Or, let's phrase the question another way: Are there any actual real-life consequences to locker room talk?

Let's talk about "priming." You know how when you're painting, you lay down a coat of primer first? Our brain does the same thing—it's constantly trying to find faster algorithms and shortcuts. Priming is the term for how talking about things in certain ways primes us to think differently—sometimes in ways we don't even notice. Some of the best examples of priming come from research done by Lawrence E. Williams and John A. Bargh, two Yale University psychologists. In one study of theirs, the researchers had participants hold either a cup of hot or iced coffee for ten to twenty-five seconds. Those who held the hot cup rated the same description of a hypothetical person "as more generous, more social, happier, better natured" than those who held the iced coffee.[7]

Some of Williams and Bargh's other studies show that people are more likely to *give* something to others after holding a warm object and more likely to *take* something if they hold a cold one, and that physical proximity affects our judgments of others. Priming affects our brains in fascinating and myriad weird ways. So, even just innocuous expressions, like, for instance, "Oh, Stephanie? Yeah, she's hot. I would definitely hit that," could help lead your brain into thinking about women as objects and sex as something you physically inflict on them. It's a jump start for building patterns in your brain. (Just to be clear here, most people who say "hit that" aren't violent. But why let your brain start to process like that?)

Actually, let's flip this. Remember David Eagleman with the fMRI study? He did a follow-up study that put people into groups based on a coin toss: heads and tails.[8] Still, people felt more empathy for those in their arbitrary coin-chosen groups than the other group—even though they knew the groups were arbitrary—so we know that creating new in-groups is simple and easy. It works even when we know that's what we're doing.

Being aware of our biases is a first step. Using priming or even outright conscious decisions, we can create and expand the groups that we self-identify and empathize with—or we can keep others out. It cuts both ways. How you use it is up to you. Transitioning away from using locker room talk isn't easy, though. It can feel like you're giving up your male relationships.

"Of course, guys use locker room talk as bonding," Bryan Stacy says. "That's the way in which guys bond. So, when we come in and we say, 'Look, stop the locker room talk, stop the porn in the office,' right? We're essentially saying: stop bonding. And these guys don't have another way to bond because they've been bonding like this for so long. They feel like there's something being taken from them."

Bryan Stacy is an interesting guy. As a Midwestern high school all-star athlete with a real talent for baseball, he thought he would go pro. That never quite panned out, so he decided to join the FBI. But then, after grueling training, that opportunity didn't pan out, either, and he had to settle for a lucrative role as a consultant (working with the FBI as a client, in poetic justice). Then, while living his life as a man's man, never-get-knocked-down kind of guy, he felt a pain develop in one of his testicles. He ignored it for a long time—a long time—and he ended up losing one of his testicles to cancer. After that happened, he decided to start a company promoting sexual health transparency. He is also the cohost of the podcast *Man Amongst Men* with Dominick Quartuccio and the cofounder of a lecture series for men, "The Discerning Dick."

"There's absolutely a better way to bond [with other men], and it's not just better because it's better for women; it's better for men, too," he says. "The major barrier is that it requires us to be open to feeling our feelings."

Stacy makes a great point, but, of course, this can be difficult to do for men who aren't used to talking about their feelings, so I called up a lot of people to try to figure out what that might look like. This brought me back to Evryman, the group Dan Doty cofounded, which hosts retreats to help teach vulnerability to men.

"Depth of relationship or depth of friendship is equal to time multiplied by vulnerability," Dan Doty says. "The vulnerability piece is what most men and most male friendships just don't [have]. You know, it's just scary."

I asked him immediately for any tips. Men are used to asking women out for dates, but most of my guy friends have no idea how to approach another guy they want to befriend.

"The first thing I would say is: admit discomfort right up front," Doty says. "An example would be, 'Hey, this is awkward, and I don't really know how to do this, but I think you're cool and I want to be friends.' Make explicit the discomfort. That's such a cool and powerful simple act of vulnerability. It just works. It's so helpful."

Dr. Niobe Way, the psychologist from NYU who has been listening to boys and men and girls for thirty years now, echoes Doty's thought.

"As humans, we want each other," Dr. Way says. "We need each other. We have the capacity to read each other's needs and wants and to connect to others—and yet there's a clash with culture that expects only certain people to do that."

Way suggests that, as a society, we box ourselves into thinking that relying on each other for emotional connection is a "feminine" trait. Men are supposed to be independent and self-sufficient and stoic. She sees this in her research time and again. Take a look at high school boys, she says. In ninth grade, they had a best friend.

In tenth grade, they had a close friend, but by eleventh grade, they called that friend an acquaintance. By twelfth grade, they weren't friends anymore.

"They explicitly talk about struggling as they get older to maintain that closeness, that intimacy. They literally articulate this [to me]. It's not an interpretation," she says. "When you're younger, as a boy, you have these close friendships, and then as you get older you're expected to give them up. Boys across the century talk about it."

Look at *Catcher in the Rye*, *Moonlight*, *Rebel Without a Cause*, and that iconic last line in the coming-of-age movie about boys *Stand by Me*: "I never had any friends later like the ones I had when I was twelve. Jesus, does anyone?"[9]

As boys become men, Dr. Way says, they're expected to compete, to rival each other for spots in the in-group. Instead of intimacy, they get alliances and pacts. In many cases, they aren't known even to those closest to them.

Remember Murray from the chapter on work—the one who tried to mentor one of his younger female colleagues? He also wanted to talk about male friendships because he thinks he's an outlier among most men. Murray has a core group of friends whom he met in university and stayed in touch with after graduation. Once a year, they take a trip to have a conversation they call "the Feels." It started one year when a friend shared that his dad had been diagnosed with Alzheimer's.

"Asking for help is okay. It's not a sin," Murray says.

During "the Feels" conversation, each person has the space to share what's happening in his life. The only rule is no shares from work. "No one cares that your manager is a dick," says Murray. The friends want only the good, deep, rich, emotional stuff. They also do frequent check-ins via Google Hangouts when someone has something going on. I asked what kind of stuff prompts a Google Hangouts chat. Recently, Murray told me, a friend was getting ready to propose to his girlfriend—but the guys had a problem with that. The girlfriend had told two of the guys in the group that she wasn't in love with their friend. Two months prior, she had even asked him for emotional space, so the guys decided to confront their friend about it and make sure he was sure he wanted to propose.

"That was really hard, but we are brutally honest," Murray recounts. In case you're wondering, the friend thanked the group for their care, but decided he wanted to go ahead anyway. And then, in a wild twist I definitely didn't see coming when he told me this story, she said yes! Despite this happy outcome, Murray is still happy they confronted the friend and made him talk through the situation. It showed everyone in the group that they were there for each other on the deepest and most honest level.

For men, the trick is building relationships based on emotional connection, rather than based on keeping someone else out. What sort of intimacy are you looking for with your friends that you're not bringing up, maybe because you're talking about a woman's nipples instead? (If you can't tell, I do not think you should ever talk about your partner's body, and I'm going to keep drilling that one home!)

RAJIV, 32

"I had two mutual friends—one guy and one girl—and the female friend of mine started showing me texts from him that just weren't okay," Rajiv says. They included things like "You're so hot" and unsolicited nude pics. When she showed Rajiv, she asked what to even say about them.

"She's very capable of standing up for herself," he says, so he thought if she is struggling with this then it's really a problem.

So he called the male friend and was like, "Hey, listen, she told me about these texts . . ."It didn't go well. The friend hung up on him twice. And then when he did get the guy back on the phone, his friend kept deflecting. "There was zero self-awareness around what he had been sending," and why it wasn't okay to keep harassing her. Even when Rajiv pointed out that it was making his female friend uncomfortable, his guy friend wasn't receptive.

Rajiv said, "Listen, until you know this isn't okay . . . until you know that, I can't talk to you."

That was the end of their friendship.

WHEN AND HOW DO YOU CALL OUT A FRIEND?

We've all got friends who say stupid shit, but in this cultural climate, it can be tricky to decide if and when to call someone out. For instance, should you still let it slide when a coworker refers to all the women in the office in a disparaging or sexist way? Do you speak up when Bob from accounting gets drunk at happy hour and talks about how bad Karen is in bed?

Rajiv's big takeaway from the confrontation with his friend was to check his own motivation. He felt good about his motive of creating a safer environment for those around him.

Jeffrey Almonte, twenty-two, who has risen to some internet fame for his YouTube videos about the intersections of race, class, and gender, had a similar confrontation experience with his "ex–best friend."

"He would try to get me to say what I did with certain women and I would kind of say, 'You know what we did,'" Almonte says. "But I was never comfortable with that because I feel like that's not just my information. That's another woman's information too."

His friend would also show Almonte naked pictures of the women he hooked up with.

"One time he showed me—like, it wasn't like a full-on nude— but he showed me a video of him grabbing some girl's ass," Almonte remembers. So he just straight up asked his friend, "Did that girl consent to you showing me that?" You can guess what the answer was to that.

Now they don't talk anymore. "That's why my ex–best friend is my ex–best friend," he says. Almonte is clear that his close circle of guy friends just don't talk or bond like that and they wouldn't tolerate anyone in their group who would. Not because of a wild, holier-than-thou feminist allegiance, but because that's just not acceptable behavior and he'd rather just call a friend out for avoiding sharing his feelings.

This went better for Jack Summers when he called out some of his friends. You might remember that Summers runs a liquor business and is also a national speaker on topics of race, politics, and culture. He's a very straightforward man and does not mince words.

"I was on a text stream with a bunch of buddies—guys who were in town, trying to figure out where we were drinking for the evening," he says. "A colleague's name came up, a female colleague, and the conversation suddenly got super sexist—borderline rape-y."

Reading through the thread, he realized his silence made him complicit and that everyone would assume he agreed with what was being said.

"So, I pipe in and I say, 'Y'all are going to make me be the mature one. I really need you to refer to our colleague in a different way,'" Jack says. "And of course the response that [I got] to that was, 'Oh, it's just jokes. It's all good!' And to that I said, 'The way you're talking about this woman now is the same way people used the N-word about you when you leave the room. It's not funny. Jokes are a prelude to violence.' That shut the conversation down."

The conversation died down, and the friendships remain.

Still, it's unnerving that the two other guys I talked to about this lost relationships over calling their friends out for shitty behavior. In general, it's tough and tricky to confront friends about this. Like when Bryan Stacy told me, "Just get your friends to open up in a more emotionally vulnerable way." And I said, "Easy for you to say!"

It turns out, it's not so easy for Stacy to say.

Stacy actually took a week after we initially spoke to talk to a lot of men in his inner circle about the best way to call out a friend without losing that friend, and this is what he came back with: "Let's say a guy has established his internal idea of what a man is, and another man crosses that boundary, friend or not friend," he says. If they decide to say something, "They're afraid they're going to get called out for not actually being that man. They're afraid that other man is going to say, 'Wait, that's not you. I know you. That's bullshit.' Like, 'Oh, are you perfect? You're saying you've never done this to a woman?' And that's the number one reason that guys don't say anything, because they're afraid they're going to be called out for their own shit."

In fact, Stacy doesn't really recommend calling others out at all. He's got a different approach.

"I'm a big believer that we have to meet men where they're at, not where we want them to be," Stacy says. "And by calling guys out and being like, 'Hey, you said that, you did that.' Like maybe there's a short-term fix, a short-term benefit. Maybe in some cases it's probably the right thing to do. But if we're talking a long-term change, each guy has to *be* it, and when each guy *is* it, they are *being* it, other guys are going to see it, and they're going to see what calling each other higher actually looks like." "Calling each other higher" is motivational speak for "hold your friends to a higher standard," by the way.

Stacy proceeded to give me an example from his own life—and I just have to say that, as someone who's known of Stacy for over a year, I was pretty surprised to hear this.

It turns out, for years Stacy used to film himself in bed with women. Some of these women were girlfriends, some weren't. All of the women agreed to be taped, but there was never a discussion afterward about what he would do with the footage.

"Over a period of years I developed this bank of ... call it self-porn, if you will," he says. "My guy friends thought it was really cool, and I thought it was really cool if I showed that to them."

Three years ago, after his testicular cancer, Stacy started to re-examine his life. "I had a really hard look at my life and saw what

[was] not in alignment anymore," he says. He decided to not only stop filming his sexual encounters, but to delete the backups. What he was doing didn't explicitly hurt the women, but he saw that it affected him—that he viewed his own sexual experiences as conquests, specifically to impress his male friends.

Now, when he goes back home to Chicago, his old friends will occasionally ask to see a tape.

"When I [say], 'Hey, I don't do this anymore,' I get mixed reactions," Stacy says. "One reaction I got was like, 'Hey, you know what, man, I'm glad you came to that.'" But that's the minority. Usually he then has to spend the rest of dinner explaining why he changed, how, and that yes, he really did delete all of the backups.

Instead of scolding and potentially ruining a friendship, he's just sharing his own personal change. He learned this from a mentor who decided to stop using the term "girls" for grown women. The mentor didn't ever chide anyone else; he just very openly talked about his own attempts to change. Slowly, Stacy couldn't say the word "girls" without thinking about it, and eventually he stopped using it, too.

"When my internal, personal desire becomes greater than the resistance or risk that's outside, that's where action happens," Stacy says. "Am I saying this because it's what society believes and I'm parroting, or because that's what I actually believe and act on?"

Some situations aren't quite as seamlessly conducive to explaining your own personal growth, though. Stacy gave another example: he met a lawyer who was second-guessing hiring a woman in the office because he liked sharing funny porn clips with coworkers.

"It's easiest for guys to connect at the lowest common denominator, because there is little risk of another guy not being receptive, and the upside of bringing something novel, exciting, or rare to the group," he says. "A safe lowest common denominator can be men's views on women, sex, et cetera, so our goal in these moments is to raise our common denominator and appreciate what the other guy is actually trying to do—maybe even spark a different conversation."

So what the hell do you do in a situation when a coworker tries to show you porn at work?

"In that moment, what can I do to allow myself to stop feeling that uneasiness when he's showing me this at work without offending this guy and telling him that he's wrong? Because that's what this whole 'calling out' thing usually is," Stacy says. "So in that moment, I don't have to go into a diatribe about women's equality and [use] all the hot buzzwords. All I have to do is tell him really simply what that's making me feel. And that's it. I don't have to tell him to do anything different."

In his case, Stacy recently underwent a ten-day porn and masturbation cleanse, and found that he was way more productive, so his sample reply would be:

"I appreciate you trying to connect with me on this. It reminds me of something I used to do. But recently, I noticed that I have more energy and seem to be happier when I stay away from porn, so this reminds me of what I used to feel like. No judgment here, it's a me thing. Let's connect on 'X' later this week."

He's doing a couple things here, which he broke down. First, he's recognizing and appreciating what the coworker is trying to do. In this case: bond. So right off the bat, Stacy is trying to make sure that isn't dismissed. Next, he's empathizing and relating. We all watch porn. They can meet each other there. Then he's providing perspective, how that's changed in his life, or what his evolving view of porn is.

There's an optional last step, which is a direct ask. It could be to wait until after work. It could be to not share porn with him specifically.

What Stacy is very explicitly not doing is judging, calling the coworker wrong, or excluding him.

"Here's the catch, though," Stacy says. "This can't be a 'line.' Just like lines come across as insincere with women, so will a line here. A guy has to be tapped in enough to state how he's actually feeling in the moment and know what made him change."

How that comes out will sort of depend on where you're at. Sometimes it may just be a kind request of "Hey, do you mind if we do or say _____ instead?" Whatever it looks like, it won't hurt to note your friend's underlying motives.

To touch on the digital streams of social media diarrhea we see from everyone, from your uncle Charlie to your ex crush in high school to your old boss, this is why Facebook and Twitter can feel like such an echo chamber of people yelling and moralizing at each other. No one can recognize the motives of a disembodied post or tweet. We see just the few pithy sentences, not the person looking for connection or validation behind them.

"It feels like one percent of the online arguments that we engage in are people actually open to having their minds changed," Colin Adamo says. "Are people actually willing to learn and grow as a result of that conversation? And it's unfortunate because it's really at a random reward interval, which is the most addictive to us, neurochemically. It really tricks us into having these conversations over and over again."

To be honest, calling out people online will probably always be less effective than exiting your browser, closing the laptop, and chucking it into the ocean. Of course, however, not all technological conversations are the same.

Let's go back to Jack Summers's story, of piping up on the text conversation. He probably could have figured out a less confrontational way to share his unease, but that's not really his style. And, as a black man, there's also the added layer of familiarity when it comes to the impact that unchecked words can have on behavior. While these friends of his maybe couldn't empathize with how their downtalk was bad to their female colleague, tying their words to the N-word was his way of making it personal for all of them.

"I realized that my voice has gravitas and that's a responsibility that I take seriously. If I speak on an issue, I'm heard and that's important," he says. His friends were able to hear him.

He's also got an interesting metric for when to speak up.

He's a straight man, so other straight men are more likely to listen to him. "It's my responsibility when women are not present to speak on their behalf," Summers says.

Here, Summers is specifically considering the feelings of the women who either are or are not present, and one of the most effective ways to communicate with your friends who are saying dumb stuff is to consider their feelings and motivations, too.

"*Most* of the time, guys haven't inspected their words, beliefs, or behavior and that's why they continue to use phrases or do things that likely offend or are just plain wrong," Stacy says. "In many of these scenarios, guys are just trying to connect with other guys."

DON, 32

Don is a sensitive soul with a deep attachment to a group of male friends he's had since college. Don isn't close with his immediate family and he's single, so this group of friends is really his support network. After some of his high school and college buddies started having babies, he moved back across the country to be involved in their kids' lives. He's a regular babysitter and can change diapers with the best of them. But he's also been feeling isolated from his core group of male friends.

They've all been close for more than a decade, but he struggles to talk about himself when they get together. "They're all just excited to be away from the kids for a bit, so it's a lot of drunken arguing and celebrating, mostly," he says. "When it's not that, like, how do you even bring up online dating to someone carrying a screaming child with one hand and cooking mac and cheese with the other?"

When his closest friend had a mental breakdown and was diagnosed as bipolar, instead of reaching within the core group to process, Don felt he had to reach outside the male group to his female friends, just to be able to emotionally process. He visits one group of female friends who live six hours away from him every couple of months.

"I always get what I call friendship hangovers after visiting my female friends," he says. "Because it's like a weekend of intense emotional vulnerability, and then I go back to my life and rarely anyone asks me questions about how I'm doing, you know?"

He increasingly finds himself seeking out the advice and companionship of women, which hasn't traditionally been the case for him. "And I guess I just worry that I'm leaning too much on my female friends," he says. "Or at least I've been thinking about how can I transfer some of the emotional closeness I get from my female friendships back to my male friends."

WHAT CAN MY GUY RELATIONSHIPS LEARN FROM MY GAL PALS?

I'm going to get to that, and I swear this all ties together in the end, but before we examine female friendships, let's look at some bleak statistics about what happens when guys don't reach out.

In the United States, in 2017, men died by suicide more than 3.5 times as often as women.[10] North American men getting a divorce are 8 times more likely to die by suicide than women getting a divorce—that's according to an overview of a whole host of studies put together by Augustine Kposowa at the University of California, Riverside. When Kposowa controlled for other factors that affect suicide rates, he put the number at 9.7 times.[11]

"Put another way, for every divorced woman that committed

suicide, over nine divorced men killed themselves," he wrote in the *Journal of Epidemiology & Community Health*.

Obviously, a lot of different things go into a trend like that, but research shows that not an insignificant chunk of the reason might be that men have fewer people to reach out to. That's true across the board and for a variety of problems. In a Mental Health Foundation survey of people with mental health problems, 28 percent of men said they had not sought medical help (compared to 19 percent of women).[12] Men are also less likely to seek medical help for physical problems, too, which helps contributes to an overall shorter life expectancy.[13]

Western ideas of masculinity tend to prize individualism and strength. Think of the lone cowboy, riding through dusty western towns with nothing but his horse, rugged good looks, and stone-eyed silence. Think of the action movie star who needs only a pistol and an attractive woman to seduce in order to single-handedly prevent global chaos.

Men often push through and decide to do it all alone. No need for a doctor, 'tis but a flesh wound. But what happens when that bleeds over to mental health areas and they need some outside help? Well, as we can see in the case of divorce, a lot of men die.

Let's go back to how traditional male friendships are structured: creating in-groups at the expense of out-groups. This can leave some men with very few places to go for more "feminine" things like, you know, talking about their feelings. In some men's cases, their only outlet for that kind of discussion is their wives, so once the marriage is severed, they have nowhere else to turn for similar connections.

There's a tweet thread I like that relates to this:[14]

> **@UR_SO_COOL_NOL**
> A woman's idea of "Let just be friends" is "Hey listen to all my problems and keep me company . . . while I have sex with someone else."

Another Twitter user replied:

> @foyinog
>
> do men understand what friendship actually is?

> @foyinog
>
> how can you complain that someone wanting to be friends with you involves doing friendship things

We've already hashed this out quite a bit, but I do want to point out that a lot of men seem to have a fundamental lack of understanding that friendships offer emotional support. Weird as it may seem, sometimes you may even find yourself becoming friends with someone who is having sex with people other than you!

"When you have men who are saying, 'How do I have friendships that aren't premised on hating women?' you have to start from 'How do you have friendships?'" Dr. Niobe Way says. "What do you want in your friends? Do you have opportunities to talk about what you want in your friendship, and do you talk about things that are vulnerable in your friendship? That's what forms a friendship. You ask questions, you talk, you ask them how they're doing. Let's talk about how you build closeness. Boys know how to do it, so men know how to do it—they've just forgotten."

I told Don that the point is not that men can't have friendships with women that are deep and emotional. The point is that men can and should also have deep and emotional friendships with men. In turn, Don told me his plan. One: make sure each of his relationships is reciprocal, that he's putting in at least as much as he's taking out. And two: try to figure out how to clear space with his male friends to be more vulnerable.

This is all to say—if it feels wrong all of a sudden when a friend of yours makes problematic comments about women, or people of a different race or class, et cetera, you're not alone. There's a cultural shift happening for a lot of people right now, and it's not the PC police. It's a conscious reckoning long overdue.

So, yeah, don't shy away from the awkward discomfort of it all. Who knows, you may even feel healthier for it in the long run, which is important when thinking about your relationship with yourself.

Chapter 7
SELF, HEALTH, AND PORN

From the ages of twenty-five to thirty, Don thought about death by suicide every day. Sometimes he would have a plan, sometimes he wouldn't. On good days, around dusk, he'd think, "Well, life won't get any better than this. Might as well end it." During depressive spells, he thought about death by suicide several times a minute.

All the while, he never sought help or talked about it.

"I dunno. I kind of always knew I needed help, but didn't know how to go about asking for it," he says. "I remember looking up therapists once and getting overwhelmed. It's not like you can compare prices and user reviews and make an informed decision. You just have to call a bunch and say, 'Here's my shit, please help.' Which is exactly what I was avoiding doing."

Don told me he'd always been taught to be tough and self-reliant. That he shouldn't lean on anyone else emotionally. When he woke up on his thirtieth birthday, Don decided that he needed to either do it and get it over with, or not. Instead, he picked a third option. "I made a bargain with myself," he says. "I'd give myself ten years. If I couldn't figure out how to live an enjoyable, fulfilling life in a decade, then I could kill myself on my fortieth birthday. I have no idea why I picked ten years. It just seemed far enough off to give me enough time to actually try."

So then Don had to actually try. He started meditating and exercising first thing every morning. He quit drinking. He decided to confront and forgive his parents for making him feel like he wasn't worthy of love when they sent him away to boarding school as a young kid. He became intentionally more open and vulnerable with friends, sometimes crying in front of them. He got a cat. Then he got another.

Don has been concentrating on how to get more of his emotional needs met from his friends. Most of his male friendships are based around arguments, usually about religion or politics, but he's trying to learn how to create the space he needs to discuss his interior life. Thus far, he says, he's pretty bad at it.

Don says he can go months now without thinking about death, which he sees as progress. But he still admits he probably needs some sort of professional help. "My brain is cracked in beautiful and tragic ways," he says.

Hello and welcome to the part of the book where we discuss *feelings*.

So far, I've written a lot about how you can upgrade your behavior for the better of society, but what about yourself? What's in it for you?

Even if you haven't had suicidal inclinations like Don, you can probably relate to feeling like you're alone with the demons in your head. This is part of the human condition regardless of gender, but I hear from men that this can come with a heightened feeling of isolation. When we as a society don't allow half the population to be vulnerable, we don't allow half the population to be healthy, right?

I want to dive into mental health. But I promise to frame it in a way that won't make your eyes glaze over.

Men don't like talking about feelings.

So much so, there's even an official term for it: Normative Male Alexithymia (NMA).[1] Turns out, there are extremely compelling reasons for why this is.

"It's more than socialization, it's biological," Dr. Helen Fisher says. "It's called emotional containment, and containing your emotions is linked with the testosterone system in the brain." (You'll remember Dr. Fisher from the previous chapters. She's the biological anthropologist who works with the Kinsey Institute and Match.com.)

Just speaking chemically, testosterone may hinder crying. And prolactin, a hormone found in higher levels in women, might encourage it.[2] In the 1980s, a biochemist named William H. Frey, Ph.D., found that women cry 5.3 times per month on average, with crying defined as anything from moist eyes all the way to bawling. Men cry 1.3 times a month. (A 2011 study found about the same numbers.)[3] And even that seems like a lot—when was the last time *you* cried? I can count on one hand the number of times I've seen the men in my life cry.

That's something I pressed Dr. Fisher on. Is there any evolutionary purpose for why men wouldn't express vulnerability? And is there any purpose for it now—in today's modern society?

"For millions of years, men did very dangerous jobs—hunting wild animals and even killing little animals to bring home dinner," Dr. Fisher says. "If you catch a little gazelle to bring it home to your family, you can't be weepy. You have to be tough-minded enough to kill the animal and then bring it home."

In other words, the men crying about killing an animal probably didn't provide very well for their families.

"You can't express fear if you're heading off to kill, to fight a war, or to kill a buffalo," Dr. Fisher says. "Vulnerability was not an adaptive mechanism for men. Men feel their emotions, and they do what's called emotional flooding. They contain and contain, and all of a sudden they erupt and get furious."

Women tend to let their emotions leak out little by little all the time, rather than remaining pent up, waiting for the dam to break, says Dr. Fisher. Does this ring true in your personal life? It does in mine.

But Dr. Fisher cautions against thinking that just because something exists organically in nature or has been happening for centuries that it's the way it should be. Actually, to the contrary. This even has a term. It's called the naturalistic fallacy. Something can be *natural* without being good or desirable. Humans have been fighting wars for millennia. Does this mean it's a good thing? No. And while both of these things exist naturally, neither is good and we should be actively trying to counteract negative impulses.

As neuroscientist Dr. Lise Eliot suggests, we as a modern society have the nasty habit of overrelying on "science" to explain away poorly socialized behavior.

To be completely honest, the way we're currently doing things isn't working out for us. Men die by suicide at more than 3.5 times the rate of women. Life expectancy is actually declining in the United States, a rarity for developed nations,[4] and according to the nonprofit, nonpartisan organization Alliance for Health Policy and news outlets like the *Washington Post* and the *Economist*, a huge reason why is what's called "deaths of despair": suicides and deaths from drug overdose and alcohol abuse. Men tend to overdose at more than twice the rate of women.[5]

The problem has crystallized to such proportions that the American Psychological Association developed new guidelines for therapists working with men and boys in 2018. Those guidelines claim that "traditional masculine ideology" harms males. (It suggests promoting other "masculinities.")[6]

Remember in the Dating chapter when I mentioned Man Box culture? Here we are seeing its worst effects.

"The constant drumbeat of male rage that floods our media and surges up in our national politics is rooted in the collective self-alienation and social isolation that defines our man box culture of manhood. The result for men is epidemic levels of divorce, depression, addiction, suicide, violence, and mass shootings," Mark Greene writes in *The Little #MeToo Book for Men*, a super-digestible and insightful book I highly recommend you take a look at. "[Men] got cheated. Yes, we did. *And everyone else is paying the price*," says Greene.[7]

We ask men to fit into an extremely narrow definition of masculinity, and when they can't, the emotions can flood out in the form of violence.

"Growing up as men, we were taught we had to be strong, tough, courageous, dominating. No pain, no emotions—with the exception of anger—and definitely no fear," Tony Porter, A Call to Men founder, explained in his Ted Talk, which has been viewed nearly 3 million times on the Ted site alone.

This is not at all an attempt to put you down. If this resonates at all for you, it's to let you know—you're not alone. This is happening on a national level.

So let's cover the ways you can manage mental health.

When I asked about mental health routines, most men I spoke to brought up physical things they do. This makes sense, since men have historically been encouraged to express themselves through physicality. But what about tending to mental health through emotional outlets? Like friends, family, and community?

You know from the last chapter that you might not have the sort of friendship with your guy friends that allows for that kind of emotional vulnerability. First, you should change that, but who does that leave? When religious affiliations were stronger, many men relied on a spiritual advisor for comfort. But in today's world that's less likely to happen, so who or what will your emotional outlet be? It's a lot of pressure to put on a significant other, that's for sure.

So, why won't Don go see a therapist still? He offered three very relatable reasons. He doesn't have health care, so there's that. He also doesn't have a lot of income, because he quit his corporate job to go freelance and therapy can be expensive. And he also admitted, he's afraid of opening up to strangers.

In this way, he's like a lot of other men.

In the United States, only about a third of people in therapy are men. Sixty percent of depressed men will seek treatment, compared to 72 percent of depressed women.

Dr. Reef Karim, a psychiatrist and assistant clinical professor at the UCLA Semel Institute for Neuroscience and Human Behavior, talked to *Mel* magazine[8] in 2018 about what keeps younger men from therapy. Women go for themselves; men go because a woman in their life prodded them to go, says Karim.

"The women we see tend to come in on their own accord, thinking, *Hey, there's something going on with me, so I'm gonna do an intake and see if I need help.* Whereas a lot of the men are coming in because of their spouse, girlfriend, or mom," Karim says. "Someone else is generally convincing them to go. We definitely see a stigma playing out."

When I asked you guys what gives? You knew this already—you just weren't totally sure how to move the needle.

> "Men are bad at self-care. They won't go to the doctor for physical needs so forget emotional needs. Part of this thing with manhood is like, 'You're a man so you need to figure it out on your own.'" —*Jeff Perera, 43, Higher Unlearning founder*

> "I think men need to be more forward about their own mental health, because the old method of just bottling all your emotions up until you die doesn't actually work and could probably be blamed for a lot of issues that we see today with bad behavior." —*Stephan Badyna, 34, A Pod Amongst Men host*

"One place we're struggling is our emotional health. Men have been conditioned to associate emotions with weakness, uncertainty. FYI, being connected to yourself is fucking scary as shit. It's terrifying. I'm sad and afraid and I have to sit and be sad and afraid and I can't do shit about it? Particularly for men who are socialized to fix things." —*Lucas Krump, 39, Evryman cofounder*

I mean, just look at the history of psychotherapy. Look back to the 1880s, starting with Sigmund Freud. Freud developed something he called "psychoanalysis" to deal with "hysterical" patients—almost all women. The idea was and pretty much continues to be that you have to be messed up and broken to seek mental help, and maybe even worse . . . be a lady!

Every time I brought up the topic of mental health or self-care for this book, I could see men's eyes glaze over. You could practically watch their thought bubbles switch channels. Some in the field of counseling are finding success rebranding "therapy" as "coaching," "consulting," or "training."[9] One man I interviewed told me I'd make more headway with guys if I referred to "self-care" as "life-hacking tips," and he was right! (Y'all do really love your Joe Rogan and Tim Ferris life hacks!)

Why is this the case, though?

"Self-care has to be called life hacking because self-care requires and is about vulnerability, whereas life hacking is about improvement and performance," Lux Alptraum says. "Look at corporations getting into meditation: It's not about meditation as being good to yourself. It's like, 'If I meditate, I will be that much more efficient and productive.'"

Liz Higgins works for Millennial Life Counseling, so she's had to consider how to best pitch therapy to this generation.

"People are realizing we can all gain from self-care and empathy, not just women," Higgins says. "That's not a feminine trait. We're going to see this unfold over time. Men are embracing emotion over physical strength, but they call it 'emotional strength.'"

Whatever its branding, attitudes toward therapy are slowly shifting. Take a gander at pop culture. Professional sports teams now bring in counselors or have them on staff, and athletes talk about viewing their brain and mentality as something to sharpen just as much as their bodies.

"I'll be in therapy. Seriously," Dwyane Wade said on ESPN when he retired from the Miami Heat after being the NBA's darling for his sixteen-year career. "I meant it; it is going to be a big change. I told my wife, I said, 'I need to do therapy, and we need to do a little bit.'

"I was always against someone that don't know me telling me how to live my life or giving me instructions. But I need someone to talk to about it. Because it is a big change. Even though I got a long life to live, other great things I can accomplish and do, it's not this. So it's going to be different."[10]

In the spring of 2018, *Saturday Night Live* aired a parody of a rap music video decked out with bling and babes, gold grills, and a Lamborghini. The chorus to the song goes: "But we gotta put in work if we want to keep on shining. We go to therapy (therapy). We spend our money on therapy."[11]

Of course, just as psychoanalysis has changed drastically since Freud in the 1880s, so too does therapy look different for this generation. In some cases, therapy is being tailored to be more results-oriented. For example, Clay Cockrell is a self-described outdoor psychotherapist, whose practice tagline is "Walk and Talk: Taking Therapy Off the Couch." For the last ten years, he's offered his therapy sessions as quite literally walk-and-talks. Clay treats both men and women, but the walk-and-talk format started because of one male client on Wall Street who just couldn't seem to make his appointments. So, Clay offered to meet the guy by his office and just do the sessions as a stroll. He noticed that his patient, whom he'd been working with for about six months, opened up on the walks.

"We men tend to have trouble with eye contact and being vulnerable," Clay says. "So there's a lot of just looking forward. And it feels less formal. There's still some stigma about going to therapy, and so just walking seems to make it easier to open up."

There's some research that indicates men tend to bond more when facing outward. Think of hunting, or riding horses together. Women tend to bond facing each other.

"I say it like this," Clay says. "Some people are bath people and some people are shower people. I don't get bath people, they sit in their gunk. Shower people wash it off, like walking therapy." At this point he's just speculating, but "[m]en are doers," says Cockrell, "so maybe the walking feels like it's allowing them to do things." I can see it.

Liz Higgins echoes this sentiment. "Men want pragmatic ways to address things," Higgins, from Millennial Life Counseling, says. "They tell me all the time in session, 'I'm a fixer. I want to fix the problems.'"

I'd caution against reading too far into observations that reduce people's behaviors to their gender—we all know plenty of men who are not doers and plenty of women who are doers. Plus, it's not like women are going to therapy just "to chat." But you can see the point they're making.

Leave gender aside entirely and part of it is just practical, right? Given the decrease in unions and full-time jobs with benefits, and the increase in college debt, many in the generation under thirty-five just can't afford to spend six years in psychoanalysis. Stints in therapy need to be shorter-term. Some are tailoring three- to six-month patient relationships.

What would it look like if you went to a therapy session with Liz Higgins? First of all, she's going to frame the session so it feels empowering to you. You're an adult; you have agency over your life and your behaviors and how you feel. She'd probably talk about "differentiation of self: developing your best self, whatever that looks like," she says. That's going to look different for each person. She'll ask you to be honest with yourself about what isn't working for you, about what you want from your relationships and to feel good.

"Honestly, from a therapist perspective, we have to kind of back up and figure out what's our leverage as therapists. What do we offer our clients?" Higgins says. "Okay, here is what I say: Why would a guy want to practice self-love? So back it up with, Okay, what do you want (as a patient)? Do you want a better relationship? Do you want to feel loved and feel good? This is what you want, right? Then start for you. . . . It ties in a lot to: focus less on finding the right partner . . . focus more on being the right partner."

"Leverage," "value proposition"—I get a kick out of talking about mental health routines in this fashion, but apparently this is the language it takes to hook some folks. Higgins is hardly the only health professional who knows they need to find the points of leverage to appeal to many men. "So what is the value proposition to men around why to do this work? I think that's the main question," says Satya Doyle Byock, a psychotherapist in Portland, Oregon, and founder of Quarterlife Counseling. It can't be so that you're not an asshole, she says. "That's not a value proposition that works for most people." (Although I will actually try to make that case in the last chapter of this book.)

Byock doesn't use the term "mental health," by the way; she calls the work she does with clients "self-inquiry." It's more in the philosophical tradition of Socrates and all the great thinkers, rather than a "you're messed up and need my help" kind of approach to therapy.

To her, the value prospect "has to be something tantalizing, titillating, attractive—something they want," she says. Byock has my attention now. Does she have yours? She encourages you to develop a better relationship with yourself because it improves your life on every measurable level, she says. For instance, it improves your health by decreasing stress, improves your general day-to-day level of satisfaction, improves levels of intimacy with friendships, increases the depth of connection with your romantic partner(s), and improves your sex life.

"Almost everything we have been taught about how to relate between genders has been wrong and fundamentally does not improve quality of life for anyone," she says.

In her practice, Higgins utilizes a concept known as "family of origin," how the lessons you learn as a child can affect the relationships you have as an adult. Sometimes that's in incredibly positive ways. Others require more examination.

"People realize as adults, *Okay, maybe the way I've been handling myself in relationships isn't the healthiest thing*," Higgins says.

Of course, the barrier to entry when it comes to therapy can be high.

"It's all so nuanced," says Mike Brown. Mike is a comedian and host of the podcast *You Good? With Mike Brown*, who waxes philosophical about the complexities of mental health. In each episode, Mike shares his journey on maintaining his own mental health and is joined by guest artists as they share theirs. "Finding a therapist is kind of like looking for a soul mate," says Brown.

To that extent, I will share that I once looked for a couple's counselor for me and my then-partner. By the time I looked up who was covered by insurance, who had openings for new patients, who didn't look like my dad, and who could meet at the few times my partner's schedule aligned with my own—there was no one in our area code. I joked to a friend that I would have paid a four-year-old to listen to our problems at that point. And we *wanted* to go to counseling.

When it comes to seeking and receiving mental health services, studies have found that in addition to gender, race and cultural reference point also plays a factor. African American men are significantly less likely to seek help compared with depressed white men, found a 2012 study published in the *American Journal of Public Health* in 2012.[12] Another 2015 study cited access, discrimination, and cultural stigmas, among other factors, for the disparity in care.[13] Asian Americans are three times less likely to seek mental health services relative to other U.S. populations, according to 2016 entry on the American Psychological Association's website.[14]

Of course, therapy isn't the only place to get this kind of help. There are other ways to do the interior work to get to emotional health.

"The platform may not even be therapy!" Higgins says. The point for men of this generation is "allow yourself to go inward," she says.

And that can be a challenge for guys who are socialized to think emotional pain is normal, not something that can and should be treated. Plus, as we know from the chapter on friendship, if you don't have a therapist, it's not likely that you express your darker emotions to your friends.

I think back to Murray's friends and "the Feels" chat every year and how rare they knew this tradition was, so much so that they had to dress it up with a name (it is a good name). Or of Don learning to cry in front of others, which he admitted is like trying to get blood from a stone.

"The system men built prevents us from being in touch with our mental health," Murray says. "So I think we have to learn to ask for help, communicate what are we facing, and stop trying to cover the sun with our finger."

When men are not allowed to be vulnerable, men are not allowed to be healthy.

So take whatever sugar you need to swallow the medicine. Rebrand it "life hacking" or find a "life coach" or skip therapy and learn to be vulnerable with friends. The comparison Higgins likes that seems to speak to some male clients is viewing the brain and heart like a muscle, and working them out the same way you would a biceps.

"It's like working out at the gym—you have to keep at it. Consistent work," Higgins says. "A male client was worried about coming to therapy, that it wasn't going to work." She looped it back to the gym. "And he was like, Okay, when I go I know I see measurable results." Gotta get those emotional gains, bro.

But here's something I've been wondering: as we promote emotional vulnerability in men, where does that leave physicality—the traditional route men have been encouraged to express themselves? Many of the responses I got about self-care made men think of the physical component.

> "Men are stuck in this belief that all improvement comes from the push: the flex of the muscle to push hard, to go faster, to do more, to work harder, to be smarter, to get it better, to do it. It's all expending energy. What that creates is a picture of a man with giant biceps and no leg muscles who can't walk. Letting go, relaxing, the reciprocal of going harder—releasing that is so impactful. What do guys do? They sit in cold water as long as they can. And that's all good, but the missing part is that letting go and relaxing and opening up is also uncomfortable." —*Dan Doty, Evryman cofounder*

> "Honestly, for me, physical labor, masculine teamwork, a healthy space for sports-person-like competition, as well as (somewhat paradoxically) restorative solitude and inner reflection all speak to me of masculine self-care." —*Clint, 32*

> "I kind of view masculinity as being a little bit more task driven, right? We like to have tasks and we do our tasks. Sometimes we do it mindlessly and we forget that other people matter. Right now, my brother was a commercial fisherman. He lost a job on his boat and his wife called me yesterday and is like, Wow, he's pretty depressed, he's out there clearing brush. So, well, you know his self-care is he's got a task to clean the garage and that's helping him feel like he's providing for his family. It probably helps him feel like he has a purpose, helps him feel useful." —*Brad, 31*

"My self-care routine is eating healthy, four to five forty-five-minute workouts every week, grooming, clean clothes, smiling, and helping others." —*Calvin, 52*

"I paint my toes, but I always have a beard. I cut my own hair, and most of the time it looks really stupid. I wear bright colors, but I'm muscular and have a strong jawline. I will never pay for a shave at a barbershop in my entire life. I don't really enjoy massages, but I moisturize and shave my armpits. I meditate and do yoga, but I also can drink 20 beers in a night hanging with my guy friends. I wake up early because the world is more quiet, but I love going to raves. Everyone is different. No one can be pegged into a slot. Some men NEED a lot of self-care, whether mental or physical; others don't. I think I'm somewhere in between." —*Jason, 30*

Here's an interesting fact: females are larger than males in most species. Think bugs, oysters, frogs, whatever—generally, the female needs a little extra heft to carry eggs. This isn't the case in humans.

Though modern society is moving in a direction toward flattening the need for men and women to be anatomically different, people born with penises have an average of 26 pounds more skeletal muscle than people born with a uterus,[15] and 30–40 percent more body strength.[16] Historically, men were even larger compared to women. Remember, in pre-agrarian society, men did all the hunting. Evolutionarily, it make sense that they'd need more muscle and bigger frames. It turns out, running after and then poking ferocious beasts with a spear is a pretty good workout.

"Men had to do their job, and it was a dangerous job protecting the group," Dr. Helen Fisher says. "It was a dangerous job bringing all these luxury items," such as meat.

So now that men don't need to hunt big game and physically fight off invaders, where does that leave your physical health, channeling aggression, and getting "swole"? Jim from the Parenting chapter is starting to think about his toddler's physical development—what he'll look like and what he'll be capable of.

"Whenever Sam hits, I think about his future power," Jim says. "Men are often physically stronger than women, and I know one thing that is clear is that you can never physically hurt a woman. You cannot use your strength to hurt someone."

Not punching people seems to be a given. What I think Jim is tapping into are different questions: How are you using your physicality? And what is your relationship to it?

"What is not totally a normal consideration at this point in culture is that our emotions are physical—they happen in our bodies," Dan Doty, the cofounder of Evryman, says.

We are all skin sacks full of chemicals. Think about it: When you work out, you release endorphins, which reduce the perception of pain in your brain and trigger a positive feeling in the body, similar to morphine. Laughter can reduce the stress hormones cortisol and epinephrine. Testosterone is involved when you're turned on, and dopamine comes when you come.

"Our approach at Evryman is equally about connecting with the body as it is with the emotions, and feeling and understanding the overlap between the two is critical and helpful," Doty says.

So, yeah, part of emotional health is physical health. Lift away. Get rippling traps, if you can. But be aware that physical health is about more than just how much you can lift.

"It also seems to be the case that repressed emotion and experience also caps men's comfort with physical modes of expression as well," Doty points out. "One of our senior guys at Evryman was a badass special forces dude that could express himself by slinging weights and breaking down doors, but couldn't be comfortable moving his body to music EVER."

Look, one of the kindest things you can do for others, perhaps even the best way to help those around you, is to take care of yourself. Be kind to yourself. Just like there's more than one way to be a provider besides making money, there's more to being healthy than just drinking protein shakes and doing pull-ups. You're a whole, complete human, which means you need attention and care to your full range of emotional needs as well as your body.

"Not to blow your mind, but men have a lot of emotions, too. What are the ways I've responded to the good things in life? The challenges in life?" Liz Higgins says. "Do I want to rewrite that script? Because you can and should as an adult. It's your life, you get to define it for yourself."

Also, maybe give dancing a try. It's fun.

And now, since we're on the topic of your body, let's talk about masturbating to porn.

NICK, 37

Nick is in his late thirties and quite high up the corporate ladder at his high-powered job. He also watches porn.

He and I have talked about his porn-viewing habits, and what he says, I think you can probably relate to. He's married and has a sex life with his wife that he's happy with, he reports. He watches an average amount of porn, he thinks. (More on how much that is coming up!) He off and on pays for subscriptions to higher-end porn sites with better production value, but his consumption is pretty mindless, he tells me. It's not a problem for him, he doesn't think. I mean, every healthy guy watches a ton of porn, right?

But, he just wants to make sure it's not eating his brain. It's not anything specific to #MeToo per se that has him wondering this, but he just a general thought like, "I watch a lot of this. Is it doing anything to me? This is okay, right?"

I DON'T HAVE TO RECONSIDER MY PORN HABITS, DO I?

I told you eventually we'd get to talk about pornography, didn't I?

Porn is a blast. It's a hoot. It's a series of other verbs that would make funny synonyms for orgasms. But there is a lot of hand-wringing about porn and the impact it's having on our generation. My inbox has been flooded over the years with concerns about porn. Some are founded, but a lot are overblown.

Let's dig in.

David J. Ley, Ph.D., is a clinical psychologist. He has a metaphor for people in his field focusing on trying to "fix" porn usage.

"If I go to my doctor and I'm sneezing, my doctor doesn't say, 'Dave, you've got a sneezing disorder. You've got to stop that shit,'" he says. "Instead my doctor tries to figure out the deeper causes and context for this."

Ley wrote the books *The Myth of Sex Addiction* and *Ethical Porn for Dicks: A Man's Guide to Responsible Viewing Pleasure*. He's a fantastic voice in the space of men's sexual health and recently gave a very insightful talk at a conference on masculinity hosted by renowned relationship expert Esther Perel.

"When sexuality issues are present, we overattend to them," Dr. Ley said at the masculinity conference. "I call this the sexual shiny object syndrome."

This "syndrome" can distract us from what the core issues are. But instead of talking about porn only as a fun fantasy (which it is!), I'd also like to examine what your usage says about you and try to help you answer the question "Why are you sneezing?"

I suppose the first way to approach this is to examine what others are doing. Just like sex, there's a lot of shame and stigma when it comes to having a genuine, thoughtful conversation about porn consumption. Sometimes it can be hard to determine if what you're doing is "normal." (Hint: there is no normal.)

What people *are* doing is—well, they're watching a lot of pornography. In 2018, there were 33.5 billion visits to Pornhub around the world. That's 92 million a day, or 207,405 every minute. There were 962 searches per second. Again, in 2018, people transferred 4,403 petabytes of data on Pornhub. I sincerely don't know what a petabyte is, but it works out to 574 megabytes per person on earth, according to Pornhub. Every minute, fifty-five people watched Kim Kardashian's sex tape.[17] And that's just on Pornhub!

Many are watching pornography gleefully.

Like when Nick found VR porn recently, he was *stoked*. But it doesn't have to be flashy stuff to enjoy it, as I'm sure you well know.

> "Porn opens your mind to the possibilities, you can explore new kinks, or find out what you're definitely NOT into. It can show you a whole world of possibilities that just might extend into other aspects of your life." —*Jason, 30*

Some are watching pornography with apathy:

> "Speaking just for myself, I know that it's just something else I use to self-medicate. Work, stress, life in general. Sometimes I just want the damn orgasm in order to relax and/ or sleep without having to tend to someone else's needs." —*Daveed, 46*

Some are watching porn shamefully.

Zachary, forty-eight, abstains because he sees it creating a "double life." There's him, then there's another secret version of him that's hiding something he's ashamed of.

"When I was a kid and I first got exposed to pornography, I was probably ten or eleven, something like that," Zachary says. "All through my teens, through my puberty and adolescence I had an obsessive relationship with pornography. That certainly colored my relationships [and] certainly colored how I saw women. Yeah, I think it's hard to escape that.

"And this was before the internet," he adds.

But back to Nick's question of whether porn is "eating his brain." Is it possible to learn bad habits from porn, consciously or unconsciously?

Remember Dominick Quartuccio? He's the cohost of the *Man Amongst Men* podcast and wrote the book *Design Your Future*. He also once went four years without watching porn.

"I didn't masturbate or watch porn for four years. When I did that, and I just started having sex with my girlfriend, it was electrifying," he says. "I could smell the shampoo of her hair and I loved to breathe in her neck because her natural body scent aroused me so intensely. I didn't need to bring in these other scenarios in my head to keep a hard-on—it was like electric."

Quartuccio's case is an extreme. He had been in Sex Addicts Anonymous because he was using sex as an excuse to avoid dealing with his feelings. This is certainly not applicable to everyone, but there really are some reasonable takeaways we should all be mindful of.

For example, "If you're getting your cues from porn, then you definitely do not know how to ask for consent," Quartuccio points out. "Choking, no condoms, no eye contact or sensitivity—those are things you have to ask for and build to."

But you'll notice I said Quartuccio didn't watch porn for four years, not that he stopped permanently. His perspective shifted over time.

"As a single dude who doesn't sleep around a lot, I am watching porn again," he says. "I believe porn has been overly vilified. It's an easy lightning rod for everything that is wrong in relationships."

With the time he spent away from porn, he developed new approaches to sexual self-satisfaction, particularly in the type of pornography he watches, and has a better understanding of why he watches it. For one, the whole sex addict thing? Yeah, he started to dig into that and learned something that surprised him.

"Research around those who identify as porn or sex addicts is crystal clear at this point: porn addicts and sex addicts are not watching more porn or having more sex than anybody else," Dr. David J. Ley says. Instead, "They just feel worse about it."

This is a critical distinction. There's not a difference in levels of porn consumption. There's a difference in levels of guilt.

"And why do they feel worse about it?" Dr. Ley says. "Because of the moral conflict they are struggling with of what they want to do versus what they were taught is okay to do."

In other words, it's not so much that you may be "addicted" to porn. You may just be ashamed. There's a pretty extreme reaction to this you may have heard of. It's called the NoFap movement. (If you don't know what NoFap means, *fap* is the onomatopoeia used in English translations of some adult Japanese manga for male masturbation. Now you can't unknow that.) It started online as a group of men challenging each other not to masturbate, and it quickly became very serious. From the NoFap perspective, abstaining from masturbating allows these folks to harness their energy, masculinity, and virility.

I don't mean to suggest there may not be underlying issues behind your porn habits that you should figure out—there might be. But porn usage that you're not happy with is probably just the symptom. Dr. Ley says that when he was a young psychologist, he was taught to have patients imagine a big red stop sign and scream "STOP" at the top of their lungs whenever they had a deviant sexual impulse. There's only one small problem with that: all the research indicates it doesn't work. In fact, it only increases the intensity and frequency of those impulses.

Dr. Ley compared this to a martial arts tactic. When facing an attack, it's much more effective to redirect a punch rather than push back directly against it.

"Behind the deviant sexual behaviors that we fear are desperate, lonely men using ineffective strategies to seek connection and safety," Dr. Ley says. "Ask men to think about their sexuality when they're not turned on. How do their sexual fantasies and behaviors make them feel? If there's shame—and I promise, there always is—that's where you plant your flag and do your work, because shame is the wellspring from which all of these things flow. Shame is what prevents men from considering these issues in the light of day."

What turns you on? What are you into? Take a moment to think about it.

Okay, now why is that? What needs do your kinks speak to?

We'll go to an extreme case, like the example of violent porn, because that's often what gets focused on in the media. (Like the sexual shiny object syndrome, as Dr. Ley has dubbed it.)

"Research shows that for about five percent of men, when they watch violent pornography, it increases the chance they will engage in sexual violence," Dr. Ley says. "It is critically important in this conversation to recognize that for ninety-five percent of men, it doesn't have that effect. We don't talk about those guys, but I think we should."

So, most likely, you're not going to enact violent pornography IRL. But you may want to consider what about it attracts you. For that 5 percent of men who do? Dr. Ley and other psychologists identify them by three factors: antisocial personalities, disinhibiting substance use, and misogyny (hatred of women).

Dr. Ley tells the story of one young man who displayed all three of those factors. He was a risk. But Dr. Ley couldn't tell him to stop watching violent porn, because he knew it wouldn't work. It would just make the man want to watch it more. So instead, they worked on the three factors: they worked through his issues of childhood abuse from the women who raised him, they brought his substance use down, and eventually the man got a girlfriend.

It took time, but the man learned how to relax and trust his girlfriend, how to make love, and how to have an orgasm. And months down the road, Dr. Ley asked him about the violent pornography.

"It's the strangest thing," the client said. "I went back to watch it, and I felt sorry for the girl in it."

"There is absolutely no research at this point that changing or restricting these sexual fantasies or violent pornography among those men reduces their risk," Dr. Ley says. "But we can reduce risk by addressing the substance use, the antisocial traits, and the misogyny."

Look, your sexual desires are probably not anything you'd need to talk to a psychologist about, or that should worry the cops if you acted on them. You're maybe into foot stuff or whatever. But it can still be incredibly beneficial to examine what lies beneath those desires.

"Porn reflects sexual fantasies and unmet needs in a person's life," Dr. Ley says.

He tells another story, of a man brought in by his wife because he was caught watching porn at work. What kind of porn were you watching? Dr. Ley asked. It was gay porn. And was he watching gay porn at work? Well, he certainly couldn't watch it at home! The man eventually realized he was bisexual. Instead of feeling shame when he was attracted to other men, he'd just think, *Oh, there's my bisexuality. Hello again.* Realizing and confronting his sexual needs turned the man into a happier, better husband—who also watched less porn at work.

As you're examining what you're into, it wouldn't hurt to consider where you get your porn. Is it one of those huge flash-based sites? What's the business model? For most people, Pornhub and other free-based porn sites are the go-to. But these sites rip videos illegally, which has a devastating impact on the actors who make them. The sites also market videos in some pretty grotesque ways. The other day, Jeffrey Almonte, the filmmaker and YouTube influencer, told me about opening his go-to site.

"I open Pornhub yesterday and the first thing I saw—I took a screenshot of it so I can tell you exactly word for word what the title of this fucking shit was," he says. "Yeah, it was like 'black guy fucks racist's wife.' And she calls him the N-word as she cries for help. I'm like, It's 2019. 2019! I'm like, bruh."

Videos like these are probably not what you want to be feeding your brain every day.

Bryan Stacy, Quartuccio's cohost on the *Man Amongst Men* podcast, had his own porn revelation after watching the controversial documentary *Hot Girls Wanted*, which takes a look at the dark and sinister side of the porn industry and its impact on young women. (It's important to note that this documentary focuses on only one sliver of the adult film world, and the worst of it.) However, this exposure was enough to make Stacy rethink his own consumption. He happened to catch the flick at an event hosted by Erika Lust. Lust is one of the leaders of the feminist porn movement. Her production company, LustFilms, employs an almost entirely female staff and works with female directors and crew. She pays her staff, crew, and actors a fair and working wage. The films themselves also feature actors of all sizes, identities, and races. There are other porn creators that focus on making ethical porn—the trick is, there's usually a membership fee.

These sites are what Stacy calls "organic, free-range porn."

"It's like the way you eat a hamburger," he says. "I'm a little more conscious what's going into that cow, how the cow is living, and therefore it's healthier for me. And I didn't recognize that porn can be kind of similar."

Now he's started to seek out other types of porn, though he freely admits there's still a hurdle.

"Here's the thing. That can all be well-known," he says. "But if it's not quick, accessible, and turns me on: Behavior is not going to change. Period."

So, sure, he may be aware that what he's watching is exploitative of the woman in it, but when he can click on YouPorn and within thirty seconds be on his way? "Like, do I really want to go search?" he says. Not when he's got a hard-on, he doesn't.

Another thing that seems obvious but is helpful to keep in mind when you're watching porn—it's not sex education. We live in a country founded by Puritans. In general, we give children shame and stigma instead of sex ed. So, there are not a whole lot of places to learn! Dr. David J. Ley likes to ask men, "Who's your sexual role model?" Straight men can't answer. Gay men can, sometimes, because they've had to think about how to integrate their sexuality, he points out. For the most part, we learn about a straight man's sexuality only when he's an abuser. Dr. Ley points out that we know more about Donald Trump's sexuality than Barack Obama's.

So when you approach porn, use it for pleasure, not for instruction. Please don't try to incorporate some random porn move you saw into your sex life. (While talking about this book, I heard from one woman that her partner was trying to choke her in bed without asking first.) Be open and honest with yourself and then your partner about what you want, instead.

"It is terrifying to express a sexual need and have the person you love reject you," Dr. Ley says. "But if you can't do that, is that an honest, healthy relationship?"

By the same token, sex educator and author Lux Alptraum cautions, "If you like porn more than your partner, think about that. Maybe it's a relationship you shouldn't be in. If you only see sex as a means to an orgasm, then you should be masturbating instead."

And maybe there are some times you shouldn't even be masturbating, either. I laughed recently about a meme I saw online that said, "You know you're an adult when you put the laundry in *before* you masturbate."

To that point, recently Stacy took a ten-day no-porn challenge. He got a ton of work done. Like, a surprising amount. It was one of his most productive weeks, he told me. He works from home, and what he realized is that whenever there's something he's dreading, he'll just avoid it by masturbating first. Now that he's reexamined his relationship with porn and figured out how he was using it as a distraction, he's better about confronting the things he needs to do first. It's been a productivity boon. It taps in a little bit to NoFap, but in a more metered way.

Your relationship with porn doesn't have to be yet another thing you hide or are ashamed of. It can help you figure out parts of your sexuality and yourself you didn't know about.

What's your porn consumption say about you? If there's shame, why is that, and what is it centered on? Do you openly talk about it with your partner and your close friends and yourself?

If you could be someone's sexual role model, what would that look like?

It may seem weird to dump therapy and porn into the same chapter, but they're part of the same conversation in my head. What are things you do daily—sit with your own thoughts and watch porn, right?

The through line on these themes is being more aware or cognizant of ways you can help yourself and not just mindlessly rolling through your life. There are so many benefits to this cultural shift happening right now, and one of them is taking the time to self-examine and upgrade.

Want a couple of life-hack and performance-boosting tips? Think of it this way: Mental health is a life hack to happiness. All this self-inquiry you're being asked to do might actually feel really empowering. You get to choose your own life! I find that idea motivating.

Chapter 8
MEDIA

Alonso went to college when he was sixteen. The son of Mexican-Americans from deep in Texas—"We didn't cross the border, the border crossed us," he says. He was the first of his family to attend college. And he'd gotten into a good one: an Ivy League university in Connecticut.

There—younger than everyone else, unread in all the things everyone else was, struggling to fit in—he often listened to music alone in his room. Especially what he called "sadboi" music, like Ryan Adams.

"*Heartbreaker*? You don't get much better than that as an album," he says.

Even as Alonso got older, figured out his place in the world, sold a screenplay, and moved into a career in media, Adams held a particular place in his Spotify library. Alonso has seen him live many times and owns all his albums.

Then in February 2019 came the allegations. According to text messages from 2014, seen by the *New York Times*, Adams was sexting under-age girls.[1]

"If people knew they would say I was like R Kelley [*sic*] lol," he allegedly wrote to one sixteen-year-old.

The *Times* reported that seven women and more than a dozen associates had described Adams as a man with a "demonstrated pattern of behavior" in which he'd dangle opportunities for career success in the music business in exchange for sex. Further, the *Times* said, he would sometimes "turn domineering and vengeful, jerking away his offers of support when spurned, and subjecting women to emotional and verbal abuse, and harassment in texts and on social media."

"I haven't listened to a Ryan Adams song since," Alonso says. "Not one."

After the Kavanaugh confirmation hearings, Alonso started examining his own life in a different way. He'd been blackout drunk at college, too. Whom had he hurt? And what was he supposed to do with his Ryan Adams fandom? The music still means a lot to him, to his evolution as a man.

"Ryan Adams, 'Come Pick Me Up,' a song I shared with an ex, someone who I felt was waaay too hot for me but I was way too on drugs for her when I was younger and cuter," Brad, thirty-six, who works in social media, remembers. "Where does that song go now?"

Most Ryan Adams fans will admit they knew he was an asshole. He doesn't hide his thornier side in his lyrics, which is part of the appeal. Here's another guy as depressed as you, just trying to figure it out. But preying on teenagers?

"Jesus Christ, that one knocked me over. I knew he was a bit of an asshole, but as the news started coming out I was having a 'WTF were you thinking, dude' moment. Texting a fourteen-year-old!" Luke D. told me. "This one pisses me off. To me he was genius. Maybe that was the problem. I am still listening to his music but it's not the same."

So, what are we supposed to do with all those songs we loved made by guys we now know are creeps?

CAN I STILL BINGE ON ALL MY PROBLEMATIC FAVES?

The meat is sizzling on the grill. The sun—and sundresses—are out. Friends and family are in the backyard, laughing and refilling tall glasses with hefty amounts of ice. Out of the portable Bluetooth speaker on the picnic table, R. Kelly's "Ignition (Remix)" comes on.

What do you do?

R. Kelly's accusations extend back as far as his hits. In 1994 he married Aaliyah Haughton, who was then fifteen. In 2002 he was indicted on twenty-one counts of child pornography (and acquitted in 2008). In the last two years, BuzzFeed[2] and a six-part Lifetime series[3] documented an alleged "sex cult," in which Kelly kept women in his home under complete control. His ex-wife says he beat her. And as of when this book went to press, he's been charged with ten counts of sexual abuse. Three of the four victims from those charges were underage. Kelly pled not guilty.

So can you still listen to "Ignition (Remix)"?

That's a tough one for Brittany Oliver, the founder of Not Without Black Women.

"My family, when it comes to R. Kelly in particular, grew up on his music," Oliver says. "He is somebody who was among the greats. He was among the Princes and Michael Jacksons. I mean like I heard his voice in my household growing up."

He makes some great music. That's true. And it's also true that Oliver is an abuse survivor.

"And so my mom and my family, we've had these conversations

about can you still listen to this person and still support survivors?" Oliver says. "I think that it becomes more complicated within black communities because he is someone who we see as a god."

She compares him to Bill Cosby. As Oliver sees it, there's a push to venerate and defend those from the black community who are producing incredible work. So much so that these two abusers managed to avoid any repercussions for decades.

"For me, because I'm a survivor of abuse, I personally cannot listen to R. Kelly's music," Oliver says. "I can't hear him when I'm at the cookout, or when I'm at an event, or anything. It's a trigger for me at this point because he's been allowed to get away with these things for two decades and no one cared. Even the black community didn't care."

However, she readily admits that not everyone is there yet, her mother and grandmother included. It's a process.

And it's a process happening with more and more men in media.

"I enjoy Louis C.K., and the first two seasons of *House of Cards* are amazing pieces of television—not to mention the impressive cultural value of Woody Allen movies," Murray, who works in international relations and has the guy group with the Feels, tells me. "So I do not stop watching any of these because I think we can separate the art from the men. I know this is a questionable approach."

A lot of the guys I chatted with spoke of separating the art from the artist.

"For me, I choose not to watch or listen to certain people if I think they're a shitty person," Stephan Badyna, the host of *A Pod Amongst Men*, says. "I have a hard time enjoying Chris Brown because I find him to be not a nice person, but some of those songs still hit hard and that gives me a real feeling of uneasiness."

Other men who talked to me would struggle to quantify the effect of listening to or watching abusers. It can be tough to pin down exactly how it affects you.

"Watching a comedian who was accused of assault doesn't make me abusive," Jason, thirty, says.

That's certainly true. Then the question becomes: How much support are you giving an abuser by watching their work?

One that's been tough for many men is Louis C.K.

Louis C.K., who has been a comedian for decades, really blew up about ten years ago with a viral clip on *Late Night with Conan O'Brien*. "Everything's amazing right now, and nobody's happy," he said, smirking.[4] A series of solid stand-up specials helped further build his public profile, including selling out Madison Square Garden not once but eight times, and his Emmy-winning FX show *Louie* cemented his place in public consciousness. In the loosely autobiographical show, it seemed like he was showing the worst parts of himself in order to examine and grapple with them.

His character talked openly of his perversions, his divorce, and his relationship with his daughters. It felt like a good guy trying to walk through the complexities of life, failing, and examining those failures to do better next time.

All the while, Louis C.K. was masturbating in front of women without their consent.

Dana Min Goodman and Julia Wolov, two comedians who talked to the *New York Times* about their encounters with him, said that his agent Dave Becky warned them to keep their mouths shut about it.[5] It was an open secret in the entertainment industry for years, before the momentum of #MeToo caught up with C.K.

After the story broke, FX canceled its deal with C.K., despite him being an executive producer of four shows on the network besides his own. HBO pulled his stand-up specials from its streaming platform.

Louis C.K. acknowledged the truth of the rumors in a lengthy apology in the *New York Times*.

So can you still watch *Louie*?

"I think that this is, in fact, a difficult question," Jaclyn Friedman, author of *Unscrewed: Women, Sex, Power and How to Stop Letting the System Screw Us All*, says. "Like, can you separate the art from the artist? At what point are you enabling them? And I don't think there's a hard-and-fast answer to this. I don't think there's a simple answer to this question, but I think that we should grapple with it."

So let's grapple.

One interesting wrinkle is Louis C.K.'s distribution model. If you're watching a show on cable, it's likely already been syndicated and paid for. But if you buy Louis C.K.'s show *Horace and Pete*, or even Tig Notaro's stand-up special *Live*, you're paying Louis C.K.'s production company directly. (Notaro broke professional ties with Louis C.K. before the allegations became public.) That feels more directly complicit than just bingeing on *Baskets*, a show made by his production company.

But even if you're just watching an old torrent of an old stand-up, Friedman points out the opportunity cost of not choosing anything else.

"We're at peak television right now. If you're watching Louis C.K., you're almost surely not watching something also tremendously great," Friedman says. "There [are] amazing, fantastic works of art that you will also enjoy, that you've not heard of because Louis C.K. is sucking up all the fucking oxygen for people who haven't abused women. And so most of the time that's what I think of. [It's like], *Okay. No, it doesn't mean that you're an irredeemable person if you like this show, but what are we missing?*"

Each Netflix view is a tacit vote. It's a sign of people giving Louis C.K. the power and access to create more.

But if you happen to like *Louie* and want to keep watching, you might be wondering, *Why pretend good art doesn't exist? Isn't that a weird masochistic punishment that helps no one? Does someone's whole life's work become void because he's a creep?*

It might be useful here to compare Louis C.K.'s work with all the shows the world will never know because the people who would have made them got bullied out of showbiz.

"What about all the women who quit comedy because Louis C.K. harassed them, right? Or they couldn't get on a bill because they declined to be in a room with him?" Friedman asks. "I'm haunted by the question of all of the voices we're missing who were harassed or abused out of creating what probably would have been your favorite shit."

You'll never get to tacitly vote for that on Netflix.

In many regards, there are a bunch of things you can do that are much more central than simply watching or not watching Louis C.K., or listening or not listening to R. Kelly. How you treat women or what you're doing to better people's lives definitely goes further than a single Spotify stream.

"The focus on R. Kelly is irrelevant, completely irrelevant to me," Brittany Oliver says. "I don't care about him and what he's doing on his own on television. I care about survivors."

She couldn't convince her mother or grandmother to stop listening to R. Kelly immediately. But that was less essential than the conversation she wanted to have.

"The first requirement that I have is not, *I want you to stop listening to him*," she says. "I'm not concerned about if someone's listening to his music. What I care about the most is are you willing to face the truth. Are you willing to understand and accept that sexual abuse and sexual violence is an issue within our communities?"

WAIT, BUT WHAT IF MY PROBLEMATIC FAVE DIDN'T DO ANYTHING ILLEGAL?

As we discussed in chapter 1, there was a narrative shift in the #MeToo movement when the Aziz Ansari story came out.

Soon after the story broke, many people started asking if Weinstein and Aziz Ansari deserved to be wrapped up in the same movement, let alone the same sentence.

"I do believe that there's a spectrum of behavior, right?" Matt Damon told ABC News.[6] "There's a difference between, you know, patting someone on the butt and rape or child molestation, right? Both of those behaviors need to be confronted and eradicated without question, but they shouldn't be conflated, right?

"I mean . . . all of that behavior needs to be confronted, but there is a continuum," he said. "I just think that we have to kind of start delineating between what these behaviors are."

The backlash got its own Twitter moment.

Even his ex-girlfriend, Minnie Driver, tweeted in response: "God God, SERIOUSLY?"[7]

"There are so many men I love who do NOT frame the differentiation between sexual misconduct assault and rape as an excuse or worse—our problem," she wrote. "Such bollocks."

In a month Damon was apologizing for his comments, and promising to "get in the backseat" when it came to the #MeToo movement.

"I really wish I'd listened a lot more before I weighed in on this," he told Kathie Lee Gifford on the *Today* show.[8] "I don't want to further anybody's pain with anything that I do or say. So for that I am really sorry."

But wait, you're wondering, what did he actually say that's so wrong?

There is a difference between some of these actions, you're muttering, and that difference is legality. Weinstein and Cosby outright raped people. That's illegal. Ansari was a bad date, you may be thinking. That's shitty, but it's still not a crime in the continental United States. Hopefully by now, you're convinced that legality isn't necessarily the best benchmark for whether or not we let behavior fly.

"I think you're asking if I believe I can separate art from the artist. Yes, and I think it's critically important for society to do so," Mitch from chapter 2 told me. "I love Aziz Ansari. I think his book *Modern Romance* brilliantly touches on how internet and particularly app-based dating has changed the landscape."

Or what about James Gunn? The *Guardians of the Galaxy* director was fired from the franchise after people dug up some really bad jokes he'd made on Twitter ten years ago. They're pretty lurid, but surely there's a difference between an immature joke and raping a woman, right? (Gunn has since been reinstated to direct *Guardians of the Galaxy 3*.)

If we toss all of these guys aside, will we be able to watch anything anymore? Is there no path to redemption?

The #MeToo movement gained mainstream attention in 2017 when actress Alyssa Milano hashtagged it. Women then began sharing their personal stories of abuse in droves in the wake of the Weinstein and Cosby accusations. It felt like an indictment of blatantly criminal activity. Five dozen women have accused Cosby of raping them. He's currently in a maximum-security state prison in Pennsylvania. Weinstein awaits trial. So when people think of the #MeToo movement, they often associate it with exposing heinous crimes.

However, the original movement was actually started in 2006 by social activist Tarana Burke. This wasn't in response to any celebrity trial. It was Burke's reply to a teenager who had been assaulted. It's a call to protect black, brown, and other women of color whose assaults are often swept under the rug. It's a way for women to share their stories and feel less isolated about the abuse they've endured. In this context, it's less about the crimes of evil men—although that was obviously part of it—and more about the solidarity of women who have had to put up with experiences from gray to outright assaults and everything in between.

Think of the Aziz Ansari story again. This time remove it from the conversation about how we should punish these men and if we can enjoy their work still and even if it's legal. Let's talk about the woman from the date. She says she repeatedly told him she was uncomfortable, and he repeatedly pushed, until he wore her down.

According to the original article on babe.net, she says she texted, "It's like nothing changed even after I expressed that I'd like to slow it down."

Should a woman on a date with a man she admires have to deal with that? Should *your* dates have to awkwardly bail and call a cab because you won't stop gesturing to your crotch on the couch? One person who thinks not is Aziz Ansari, a year later. He talked through his change of heart in a stand-up show, as reported by Vox February 2019.

"But you know, after a year, how I feel about it is, I hope it was a step forward," he said. "It made me think about a lot, and I hope I've become a better person." According to Vox, Ansari said a friend had told him that Ansari's situation made him rethink his own dating life. "If that has made not just me but other guys think about this, and just be more thoughtful and aware and willing to go that extra mile, and make sure someone else is comfortable in that moment, that's a good thing."

Ultimately, the #MeToo movement is less concerned with what to do with Ansari and is more concerned with what we do for his date. This is a conversation worth having.

I can't point to a specific act and say, "You can do this but you can't do this." I can't tell you that it's okay to watch Celebrity X but not Celebrity Y. No one can. But you know what rape is and you know what consent is, especially now. For everything in between, you're going to have to grapple with each individual case and decide for yourself what's okay in your own life. All of us are. It's definitely not clear-cut.

Islam has a beautiful way to tell night from day. During Ramadan, observing Muslims fast during the day, "and eat and drink until the white thread becomes distinct to you from the black thread at dawn" (Quran 2:187). That's a distinct moment in time, when there's enough dawn light to distinguish between a white thread and a black thread. There's no similar blanket rule for most of the of the stories we've talked about here.

For example, Dave Chappelle tried to figure out what to do with his idol Bill Cosby in a bit during a 2017 Netflix special. He started off by explaining history from World War II on, about women entering the workforce by the millions, the political assassinations of the 1960s, and the wild '70s. "And while all this was going on, Bill Cosby raped fifty-four people," Chappelle said. "Holy shit, that's a lot of rapes, man. This guy is putting up real numbers. He's like the Steph Curry of rape. Man, that's a lot of rapes: fifty-four."[9] (At the time, there were fifty-four allegations against Cosby. There are more now.)

He compared learning about Bill Cosby to hearing that chocolate ice cream itself assaulted dozens of people. But he also still remembers why he idolized Cosby in the first place.

"I've never met Bill Cosby, so I'm not defending him. Let's just remember that he has a valuable legacy that I can't just throw away," Chappelle said. "I remember that he's the first black man to ever win an Emmy in television. I also remember that he's the first guy to make a cartoon with black characters where their lips and noses were drawn proportionally. I remember that he had a television show that got numbers equivalent to the Super Bowl every Thursday night. And I remember that he partnered up with a clinical psychologist to make sure that there was not one negative image of African-Americans on his show. I'm telling you, that's no small thing. I've had a television show. I wouldn't have done that shit. He gave tens of millions of dollars to African-American institutions of higher learning, and is directly responsible for thousands of black kids going to college—not just the ones he raped."

Bill Cosby is in jail. Some of the people he inspired are doing Netflix specials or using the college degree he paid for. People are complicated.

Less complicated is the idea that women shouldn't leave dates in tears and feeling violated. How do we get to the point where that's the case? And what can you do to help it along?

WHEN CAN MY PROBLEMATIC FAVE RETURN?

When Louis C.K.'s habit of pleasuring himself in front of women became *New York Times* public, he issued a statement.

"These stories are true," he wrote.[10] "At the time, I said to myself that what I did was O.K. because I never showed a woman my dick without asking first, which is also true. But what I learned later in life, too late, is that when you have power over another person, asking them to look at your dick isn't a question. It's a predicament for them."

He then removed himself from the public view to consider his actions.

"I have spent my long and lucky career talking and saying anything I want," he wrote. "I will now step back and take a long time to listen."

That self-imposed exile lasted about half a year. Then he started making unannounced appearances back at the Comedy Cellar in New York. A few months later, some of his new jokes started to surface online. His new material made fun of the kids who survived the school shooting in Parkland, Florida.

"You're not interesting because you went to a high school where kids got shot," C.K. said. "Why does that mean I have to listen to you? How does that make you interesting? You didn't get shot. You pushed some fat kid in the way. Now I gotta listen to you talking?"[11]

He complained that a very offensive word for people with mental disabilities isn't PC anymore. And he imitated trans people: "You should address me as they/them. Because I identify as gender neutral," he said. "Okay. You should address me as 'there,' because I identify as a location. And the location is your mother's cunt." Okay.

He got booed, audience members walked out, and his later performances, which were advertised, had protesters outside. I think we can presume they were protesting more than just how bad those jokes are.

So then the question becomes: When can these guys come back?

There doesn't seem to be a consensus. It's not like there's an online class these abusers can take and then they're cured and allowed to come back into popular culture. So if you're waiting until you're allowed to put "Ignition (Remix)" back on your "BBQ vibezzz" playlist, it's hard to estimate a time frame until you won't get scowls. A big part of that is the core reason why these guys have been run off from their jobs in the first place.

Let's look at Charlie Rose, for example. The former CBS News and PBS host was accused by a few dozen women of sexual harassment, including groping and exposing himself to direct subordinates. What is the appropriate penalty for him? This is what we are still figuring out, but the #MeToo movement is less about punishment. It's more about preventing these abuses in the future. So could your boycott play a role in that?

Charlie Rose getting fired because of these allegations means he can't keep putting coworkers in the position of withstanding sexual harassment in order to keep a job—for now. Louis C.K. is free to keep traumatizing nonconsenting women, but now he will have more difficulty threatening their careers if they talk about it.

"Listen, I'm not saying Louis C.K. should never work again—he can always go work in McDonald's or something," Lux Alptraum says. "But he shouldn't have a platform that gives him access to power, because he's shown that he's wielded that power wildly inappropriately."

That's a main goal of the #MeToo movement: separating abusers from power with the ultimate goal of preventing these abuses from happening in the future.

CAN YOU LIKE PROBLEMATIC CONTENT?

All of that is just one side of the question, though—art created by people who are abusers IRL. The other side is: What about art created by probably fine people that is in itself troubling? It's not like you can agree with everything you watch and listen to.

"Listening to a rapper who says 'fag' doesn't make me a bigot," Jason, the butcher who is going to stay home with his kid, tells me.

But then where is that line? Again, it's unclear, so I called up Ashley Lauren Rogers, an actress and director who also hosts a podcast called *Is It Transphobic?*, to ask.

"I don't know where it comes from, but I absolutely love terrible movies. I love terrible media. And a lot of that sort of veers into problematic areas," she says, chuckling. "It just makes me laugh because I know it took so many levels of people and producers and writers and so many people, and the product is so bizarre, that I just can't help but love it. . . . Part of it is you have to laugh so you don't cry, but the other part of it is, like, I'm laughing at this way longer than I think I should be."

She started her podcast after a lengthy argument with a friend about the movie *Dallas Buyers Club*. Rogers, a trans woman, didn't want to bother watching it, because she figured she already knew how it would get things wrong, based on how Jared Leto was talking about the film in interviews. Her friend argued that she couldn't prejudge the movie before she'd sat through it. Then Rogers started a podcast about watching all these terrible movies—so you don't have to.

"I can always tell: Yep, there were no trans people in the writing room. There's no nuance. And I think that's what it comes down to: I can tell because there's such a lack of nuance," she says. "Why does it matter if there's nuance? It matters because, broad strokes, it creates the idea that there are no trans people in real life, and that there's just this concept of trans. It reduces this group of people, trans people, to specific factors that keep them from being human, and lock them into an idea."

Rogers pointed out plenty of other examples of media, not necessarily problematic for their portrayal of the trans community, but for other iffy material. For example, she loved *Scott Pilgrim vs. the World* the first time. But when she went to rewatch it, years later, she couldn't finish it. A central plot point is Scott Pilgrim dating an underage girl. She also had to quit watching *Game of Thrones* when she became uneasy with all the nonconsensual sex that hadn't been in the books.

There are other things she admits are troubling as hell but that she happily watches.

"I think when media is problematic, you can make a choice," she says. "Either it is affecting you in such a way that you say, 'I need to walk away from it,' or you say, 'Yeah, I'm okay with watching this. I'm okay with this because it's a piece of fiction, it's a piece of media.'"

How much does the media we are watching imprint on us? There's definitely not a one-to-one relationship between seeing media and believing it, or it having an impact on how you behave. But it can influence what we see as acceptable social behavior.[12]

One very dark example is the influence a celebrity death by suicide can have on the public. After a celebrity dies by suicide, studies have shown people are fourteen times more likely to attempt death in the same manner.[13] The month Marilyn Monroe died by suicide, August 1962, suicides spiked by 12 percent. In fact, there are now guidelines for how news outlets cover suicide—including not listing the manner of death and not putting "suicide" in the headline. The point is, media can affect what we see as important. For instance, you seeing media about the #MeToo movement probably contributed to you picking up this book. Again, none of this is direct or one-to-one. It's fuzzy at best.

Whether or not you still watch questionable media, or engage with material put out by questionable people—these decisions are going to be on a case-by-case basis for each individual person. Rogers still sometimes recommends *Game of Thrones*, but she definitely doesn't recommend it to survivors. And Rogers doesn't have any answers beyond just thinking through this stuff as much as you can.

"In what ways can we reduce the harm and still be okay with the media?" she says. "I think that's a question that we don't know how to answer."

But like everything in this book—just because we don't have an exact answer doesn't mean we get to ignore it. We can't always tell the difference between the color of thread, but we know what white thread looks like and we know what black thread looks like.

"I think it's impossible to be a purist about these things," Jaclyn Friedman says. "But I also think saying, 'Well, we can't be a purist, so why bother thinking about it at all' is a cop-out. It's a spineless cop-out."

And so, the question is now—where do we go from here?

Conclusion

WHERE DO WE GO FROM HERE?

CLEO, 32

I met him at a landmark hotel in midtown Manhattan, where he was staying. We grabbed a drink at the bar.

I was a junior reporter still trying to prove myself on camera. He was a senior producer at the network where I worked. He'd texted to find out if I'd want to meet and chat about story ideas we could potentially work on together. In media, like many other industries, business is not relegated to conference rooms. Many relationships and thus deals are forged off-site at drinks, dinners, or events.

We talked about a big international story idea I would report for his show. The exposure would be big for me, and an opportunity to flex my reporting chops. If I got this assignment, who knew where my career would go?

Then he kissed me and asked me to come upstairs to his hotel room. I pushed him away, said no, and left. I wasn't attracted to him. But that's not really the point in these situations. He had way more power and influence than I did. To me, this was business. But to give you a sense of how common it is for women to be hit on by male colleagues, it did not even cross my mind to report him. I was disappointed and aggravated by how that conversation had ended, but I was not shocked.

Instead, I waited a couple of days for things to blow over and then followed up over email about the potential story idea we had discussed, as if nothing else had happened. He never wrote back or responded to any more of my emails. That opportunity was dead in the water.

I always wondered how my career would have been different if I had gotten that opportunity.

WHERE DO WE GO FROM HERE?

That story happened a couple of years before #MeToo. A couple of years before that, when I got my first job in journalism, I worked at a financial news network. As a junior producer, I would shoot small TV spots in a secluded camera wing right after one of the world's most famous journalists would shoot his. Everyone always warned, "Don't be alone with him!" And though nothing untoward ever happened between us, the whisper network about this guy was in full effect. And no, I don't remember anyone ever *thinking* about reporting him. A legend in the industry, this man has since lost his prominent job, having been linked to serial sexual harassment and abuse scandals at work in the #MeToo reckoning.

A couple of years before that, I had worked as an administrative assistant at a biotech investment firm straight out of college to pay off student loan debt. I had aspirations of one day being a financial analyst myself and wanted to see if I liked the industry. (I would have been terrible at that job and, nope, I hated it.) In this office of almost entirely male associates and partners, one boss explained a formula to me for calculating a financial concept known as "depreciating value" in terms of my own depreciating desirability as a woman in my early twenties, having hit my peak appreciation (that is, hotness) around nineteen, he said. He drew a chart to show me how, by contrast, men like him had "appreciating value" as they advance in age, in their careers, and in status.

Another one of my bosses there, a happily married man with a kid and another on the way, showed me the viral video "Two Girls One Cup." (If you haven't seen it, spare yourself.) And although the firm was legitimately invested in a company that manufactured breast implants, some male employees (including the CEO) kept the implants on their desks for seemingly no other reason than to be able to talk about breasts casually in the office. While most of the employees there were perfectly nice, last year the CEO was forced to step down amid sexual harassment claims in the #MeToo culling.

That's three for three if you count them. Three sequential workplaces, three weird work atmospheres. I also do not consider myself in any way to be "a victim"—I'm just a woman in America in 2019. In fact, as a white straight woman, I have an extraordinary amount of privilege, which I realize with crushing awareness every time I go on Twitter for daily headlines.

That is to say, when #MeToo started to unfurl, I, like many women, felt like a cork about to pop. On the one hand, it's been validating to hear others openly share similar experiences. But I knew I wasn't alone. We all knew this was happening; it was barely concealed under the surface. On the other hand, it's been frustrating to hear many claim that the #MeToo movement is overblown or going too far. It's not just men who say this, either—women do as well, and especially women my mother's age, like the publicist in her sixties who recently pulled me aside to say, "I can tell you're the type of woman who doesn't take any shit, but let me just tell you, me and my friends think this *whole thing* is kind of ridiculous. In my day, every boss I had tried to put their hands up my skirt."

The fact that things have gotten better for some of us doesn't mean we should stop improving for the rest of us.

I've mostly stayed away from publicly commenting on my own #MeToo experiences, since I see my role as a journalist is to report other people's stories, not my own. What's made me jump off the sidelines and into the public #MeToo conversation is men. You guys.

From my vantage point, there are so many incredible women speaking to women and #MeToo survivors. But these spaces have been facilitated mostly by and for women and queer-identified folks. You can rarely find a straight dude in sight. Where are all the men? Where is the support from the "good guys"? After many emails, DMs, and private conversations, I realized that the passion and fury of many voices in the #MeToo space have left a lot of men feeling too uncomfortable to get involved.

I recently grabbed drinks with three male venture capitalists. When discussing my book, they all remarked, "This whole thing really just makes you not want to hire women. But we don't *want* to feel like that!" These men (and many men) have huge hiring power. As a society, we cannot afford to have them privately feeling gunshy about hiring half the population.

At a certain point, it got very depressing to hear from so many of you that we could be missing a great opportunity to call you in, work together, listen to each other, and make changes. After all, I've learned from talking to you guys for this book that you feel like things are working against you too. So, let's at least fumble around together trying to move in the right direction.

The fact is, everything we're talking about has been happening for decades, at least. "Harvey Weinstein began this conversation, but it's not a new conversation," Jessica Bennett, the *New York Times* gender editor, told Vice News.[1] "I think a lot of us, all genders, are looking back on past experiences with a new lens now and you can't really put this back to the way it was."

Of course, men are not the only ones critical of the #MeToo movement. Michelle Hope, the sexologist you met in chapter 2, recently told Vice News, "I sometimes become frustrated that the #MeToo movement has moved so far away from what it started as—an opportunity for us to call attention to youth of color and disenfranchised communities that experienced physical assault. And now it's like, 'Is Aziz Ansari guilty, really?'" This is a sentiment I heard from many of you as well.[2]

It's this exact question—*Where do we go from here?*—that has me working on this book with all of you.

Here's the thing: No one has the answer to this question. There's no clean solution. At best, we're looking at a decade's worth of very uncomfortable conversations and situations. But that doesn't mean that what's happening is bad. In fact, as I've said, it's way overdue. This is an opportunity to build a better society for all of us.

Austin, the successful businessman and avid porn enthusiast, told me that even though the intricacies of what's happening right now scare him, in principle he's in favor of #MeToo and all the changes because he's in favor of "progress and advancement on a social level" in general. He sees progress as a path to equity. "For societies to improve they have to progress," he says.

So how do you resolve centuries of conflict and inequity? The short answer is that you have to strap in for the long haul.

WHAT IS YOUR ROLE IN ALL OF THIS?

Tony Goldwyn, the actor from *Scandal*, told me about a private, hush-hush meeting that he attended with a bunch of male Hollywood actors and producers after #MeToo and Time's Up gained momentum. I asked him what his most interesting observations from the meeting were.

First, he was alarmed when the facilitator opened the event by saying, "The good thing is the majority of you, eighty-five percent of you, are good guys and you're not abusers or rapists." Goldwyn tells me he was horrified: "I was like, wait, fifteen percent of us *are*?! What the hell! And it freaked me out." Yes, it's definitely a weird time when you can pat yourself on the back because *only* one out of every seven of you is an outright scumbag.

Goldwyn was also bothered by the indignant reactions. "A lot of guys had this sort of sense of outrage that pissed me off," he says. "They were like, 'Oh, well, you know this isn't a crime. . . . You know, guys—we're not allowed to do anything anymore!'" One person said, "You know, behaving boorishly is not a criminal offense."

This pissed Goldwyn off. That isn't the point! Yes, being an asshole might not get you convicted of a crime, but "it's just that there's a sort of sense of entitlement buried in that—a lack of taking of responsibility or really introspection," he says.

On the other hand, there's a real sense of fear that Tony relates to. One well-known actor stood up and said, "You know, I want to be an advocate, but I'm afraid . . . as a celebrity." Tony says, "He was a very famous guy that said, 'If I start speaking out, I'm worried someone's gonna say something about something I did twenty years ago that either I didn't do, or I didn't even know I was doing it at the time. And that could take me down—that could ruin my life because of what's happening now. Like that could destroy my career and my reputation. I'm so scared.'"

It's a conundrum. How do you help without putting yourself at risk in the process?

Goldwyn tells me that he's had to reconcile a lot of his own behavior. For example, he's a hugger. He's very physical and always has been, and had never thought twice about being affectionate with the women he knows—colleagues, friends, etc. Since #MeToo, he's considered what it means that he never stopped to think that some women might not appreciate it.

"You know this thing of all these men being like 'I'm a great guy'?" he says. "You have to really ask yourself, 'What am I doing in my behavior?' It's about being conscious."

Bryan Stacy, from the *Man Amongst Men* podcast, has a similar idea for incremental improvement. Remember his mentor who decided to stop using the term "girls" for grown women? No lectures, just an open desire to improve, wore off on Stacy as well.

Catalog your own behavior. Make incremental changes within yourself. Then hold yourself and others accountable.

HOW DO YOU ADMIT WHEN YOU'VE CAUSED HARM?

If you've made it this far, you might have done some inner cataloging and realized that somewhere along the way, you may—okay, let's be real, you probably *have*—been complicit in some of this messed-up stuff. You may want to think about an apology. But saying you are sorry and opening up a conversation may seem too scary or too high-risk for not enough reward. Let me try to convince you otherwise. (Again, in this book, we're not dealing with violence, severe brutality, or criminality. I'm referring to "the gray areas," the behavior that might not be *illegal*, but still has the potential for harm.)

There's one apology that stands out. It came from Dan Harmon, the creator of *Rick and Morty* and *Community*. One of the former writers on the show *Community*, Megan Ganz, called him out on Twitter for sexual harassment. As a response, Harmon went on his podcast to give a fifteen-minute monologue indictment of himself.

"I drank. I took pills," he said on *Harmontown*.[3] "I crushed on her and resented her for not reciprocating it, and the entire time I was the one writing her paychecks and in control of whether she stayed or went and whether she felt good about herself or not, and said horrible things. Just treated her cruelly, pointedly. Things that I would never, ever, ever have done if she had been male and if I had never had those feelings for her. And I lied to myself the entire time about it, and I lost my job. I ruined my show. I betrayed the audience. I destroyed everything, and I damaged her internal compass."

He had a crush on Ganz for two years, broke up with his live-in girlfriend because of it, and kept telling Ganz he loved her.

"I certainly wouldn't have been able to do it if I had any respect for women," he said. "On a fundamental level, I was thinking about them as different creatures. I was thinking about the ones that I liked as having some special role in my life. And I did it all by not thinking about it. So, I just want to say, in addition to obviously being sorry . . . I want to say that I did it by not thinking about it and I got away with it by not thinking about it."

Recently, the popular podcast series *This American Life* profiled Harmon's apology.[4] Others in the advocacy space have written about why his apology meant something, as opposed to the empty, stuttering non-apologies we've seen from others.

Ganz is now an executive producer for the comedy series *It's Always Sunny in Philadelphia*.

"Here's a weird one for you: Last week, I called out my former boss @danharmon for sexual harassment, and today I'm going to ask you to listen to his podcast," she tweeted, upon hearing Harmon's apology.

"[It's] ironic that the only person who could give me this comfort is the one person I wouldn't ever ask," she told *This American Life*.[5] "It is a master class in how to apologize. I only listened because I expected an apology, but what I didn't expect was the relief I'd feel hearing him say 'These things actually happened.'"

So, that's a famous guy who went big and public with his apology. But this is happening on a much smaller scale, too. Remember Alonso, the R. Kelly fan from chapter 8? He told me the story of his own apology process.

As mentioned in chapter 8, the Kavanaugh hearings really hit home for Alonso. A graduate of Yale himself, he remembered his own college times as somewhat dark. "I drank a lot in college, so probably if someone said I had a drinking problem, I couldn't dispute that. And I'd like to say with ninety-nine percent certainty that I never did something inappropriate. The reason I say ninety-nine percent is because there's like definitely one percent I can't remember because there were nights that I blacked out."

Specifically, Alonso remembers one woman that he hooked up with only whenever he was drunk. He's not proud of their interactions. They're still Facebook friends, but they haven't spoken in years. He messaged her recently and apologized if he ever made her feel "less than."

"I wasn't expecting forgiveness or absolution," he says, "but I wanted to say it." She hadn't been expecting his apology, but she was appreciative and thanked him.

Some women may be less receptive. Forgiveness is its own process. The apology—and making sure you never have to apologize for something similar again—is yours.

WHAT IS RESTORATIVE JUSTICE?

There's a concept I want to introduce you to called restorative justice. The theory behind restorative justice is a view of crime as more than just breaking the law. "It also causes harm to people, relationships, and the community," according to the organization Center for Justice and Reconciliation.[6]

"A society that measures justice only in the length of a prison term is limited in the possibility of achieving change and reducing harm," write Alissa Ackerman, Ph.D., professor of criminal justice at California State University, Fullerton, and Jill S. Levenson, Ph.D., a law professor at Barry University in Miami, in a 2016 piece for *Psychology Today*. "Instead, we look at the flaws in our process that prevent true healing for survivors and preclude opportunities for perpetrators to play a role in promoting prevention, empathy, and accountability."

Basically, the practice of restorative justice can look different depending on the situation, but there are three key components that stay the same. One: that the person who inflicted the harm acknowledges the full extent of the harm they have inflicted. Two: that repairing the harm is a cooperative process between the people most affected, and especially the survivor. And three: that the process ultimately yields an understanding and transformation on the part of the person who has inflicted the harm to ensure they do not continue this harm to others in the community.

Traditionally, restorative justice processes have been reserved for minor offenses, but some school programs are introducing it with peer-to-peer councils. With regard to Brock Turner, the Stanford student who was convicted of raping an unconscious woman, Ackerman and Levenson offer tips for reimagining how we think about harm and trespass:

"What if we lived in a culture where Brock was encouraged to authentically take responsibility, and to express his remorse directly to the victim for causing her suffering? What if he was able to articulate his comprehension of the many ways in which his actions initiated a cascade of emotional consequences for her? What if he were required to pay for her medical costs and psychological counseling? What if, instead of offering to teach college students about the dangers of drinking too much, he was sentenced to creating and providing (at his own expense) educational programs for college students about consent, respect, healthy sexual boundaries, and the damaging impact of any unwanted sexual contact? To us, these sound more like sanctions that could change the world, and the survivor, and Brock, for the better."[7]

Law professors and social justice advocates are not the only ones putting careful thought into what it means to reconcile and move forward in our current situation. Rabbi Danya Ruttenberg wrote for the *Washington Post*[8] about what Judaism can offer us in the wake of #MeToo. "The Jewish tradition teaches that repentance is really hard work," she says.

There's a specific Hebrew word for the work that goes into repenting: *teshuvah*. "The bad actor must own the harm perpetrated, ideally publicly," she explains. "Then they must do the hard internal work to become the kind of person who does not harm in this way—which is a massive undertaking, demanding tremendous introspection and confrontation of unpleasant aspects of the self. Then they must make restitution for harm done, in whatever way that might be possible. Then—and only then—they must apologize sincerely to the victim. Lastly, the next time they are confronted with the opportunity to commit a similar misdeed, they must make a different, better choice."

It's a multistep approach with no expectation of forgiveness, which might feel severe or even scary.

"You can't avoid the conversation because you're uncomfortable— that's the definition of privilege,"[9] says Brené Brown in her recent Netflix special *Brené Brown: The Call to Courage*. Brown is a research professor from the University of Houston who studies shame and courage and whose Ted Talk on vulnerability is one of the most popular Ted Talks of all time. "You have to choose courage over comfort. So, all of us need to allow for vulnerability and imperfection. It's required," she says.

And Dr. David J. Ley, the clinical psychologist and expert in male behavior and ethical porn consumption, says, "We have to ask ourselves, do we want revenge, or do we want change? We only get to choose one."

Look, what we think of as "traditional" gender archetypes and gender roles aren't working for many of us. We know they don't work for many women, femme, and nonbinary folks. And having done nearly a hundred interviews for this book, I can tell you they aren't working for many men, either. My biggest hope for all of us is that we start to take heed of the changing times and shed aspects of the gender binary that no longer serve us. We know from neurology and anthropology that gendered behavior is predominantly a matter of socialization and that many of our traditions hark back to a time and way of life that no longer exists.

Genderqueer, nonbinary, trans, and queer folks have long been doing the work that many of us straight cis folks are just starting to reckon with, and they've learned invaluable lessons about how freeing and authentic it can be when we live outside outdated prescriptions. (They also pay the highest price for this with higher rates of discrimination and violence.)

"One of the greatest gifts of my transitioning from female to male has been to see the constancy of who I am throughout life," Alex Schmider, the media whiz at GLAAD, says. "My masculinity has always been rooted in being a protector, defender, and leader—all of which were with me before embracing my true gender."

Schmider suggests you do the following exercise: Think about someone who has protected you, provided for you, led you. Do you see a gender? Or a person? "Ultimately, would their gender matter if they were still the same person?" No, it would not.

I do not agree with everyone I interviewed for this book, but I deeply empathize with the confusion and fear right now. I wish we could find it in ourselves to be less defensive and more earnest in our efforts to make our immediate communities better places.

I honestly think the first step is to hold unexamined behaviors up to the light—to rethink the actions you've never thought about and prefer to never think about.

It's complicated, it's uncomfortable, and it won't happen overnight. There are no shortcuts.

Acknowledgments

This book is a community project and a community effort. It belongs especially to those who willingly shared their experiences with me—I'm truly honored you trusted me with your stories.

I'm also particularly grateful for the wonderful team around me:

Thank you to Zac Rigg, a masterful writer and creative brain. I couldn't have done this book without you.

To my manager, Liz DeCesare, my constant champion and voice of reason.

To the Simon & Schuster team and Tiller Press imprint—my editors Lauren Hummel and Anja Schmidt, and Theresa DiMasi for the support and opportunity.

To Sam Ford for believing in me on this project and many others.

To Lux Alptraum, a brilliant mind. I always feel better with you in my corner.

To Danielle Friedman, the gold standard when it comes to reporting, editing, and publishing.

To Haylin Belay and Lauren Gerber for their research assistance and Diana Crandall for fact-checking.

To my parents, Jamie Stiller and James Farrell, for coaxing me on and always believing in me. I am forever grateful to you. And the countless friends and family who encouraged and supported me during this project.

Notes

Introduction

1 Jackson Katz, "Why We Can No Longer See Sexual Violence as a Women's Issue," interview by Guy Raz, *TED Radio Hour*, NPR, aired February 1, 2019, https://www.npr.org/templates /transcript/transcript.php?storyId=689938588.

Chapter 1: **DATING**

1 Moira Weigel, *Labor of Love* (New York: Farrar, Straus & Giroux, 2016).

2 Tony Porter, *A Call to Men*, filmed in 2010 at TedWomen 2010, https://www.ted.com/talks/tony_porter_a_call_to_men ?language=en.

3 Paul Kivel, *Men's Work: How to Stop the Violence That Tears Our Lives Apart* (Minnesota: Hazelden, 1992).

4 B. Heilman, G. Barker, and A. Harrison, *The Man Box: A Study on Being a Young Man in the US, UK, and Mexico* (Washington, DC, and London: Promundo-US and Unilever).

5 Isabel Thottam, "10 Online Dating Statistics You Should Know," eHarmony.com, accessed June 2019, https://www .eharmony.com/online-dating-statistics/.

6 Jack Peat, "Millennials Spend 10 Ten Hours a Week on Dating Apps," *Independent*, January 23, 2018, https://www.independent

.co.uk/life-style/dating-apps-millenials-10-hours-per-week
-tinder-bumble-romance-love-a8174006.html.

7   Yael Bame, "53% of Millennial Women Have Received a
    Naked Photo from a Man," October 17, 2019, https://today
    .yougov.com/topics/lifestyle/articles-reports/2017/10/09/53
    -millennial-women-have-received-dick-pic.

8   "Trends in the Prevalence of Sexual Behaviors and HIV Test-
    ing," National Youth Risk Behavior Survey 1991–2015, https://
    www.cdc.gov/healthyyouth/data/yrbs/pdf/trends/2015_us
    _sexual_trend_yrbs.pdf; Kate Julian, "Why Are Young People
    Having So Little Sex?" *Atlantic*, December 2018, https://www
    .theatlantic.com/magazine/archive/2018/12/the-sex-recession
    /573949/.

9   Matthew Hussey, "Who Pays on a Date? Men or Women?"
    accessed June 20, 2019, https://www.facebook.com/watch/?v=
    1214771905208544

10 Eileen Patten, "Racial, Gender Wage Gaps Persist in U.S.
    Despite Some Progress," Pew Research Center, July 1, 2016,
    https://www.pewresearch.org/fact-tank/2016/07/01/racial
    -gender-wage-gaps-persist-in-u-s-despite-some-progress/.

Chapter 2: **SEX**

1   Katie Way, "I Went on a Date with Aziz Ansari. It Turned into
    the Worst Night of My Life," Babe.net, accessed June 20, 2019,
    https://babe.net/2018/01/13/aziz-ansari-28355.

2   Frank Andrews, Yelena Peigne, and Judith Vonberg, "Catherine
    Deneuve Denounces #MeToo in Open Letter," CNN.com,
    January 11, 2018, https://www.cnn.com/2018/01/10/europe
    /catherine-deneuve-france-letter-metoo-intl/index.html.

3   "Straight men would have so much more sex if they just treated
    their casual sex partners with the tiniest modicum of respect and
    human decency," Twitter, December 12, 2018, https://twitter
    .com/LuxAlptraum/status/1072888586586996736.

4   Sophie Lewis, "'Consent Condom' Requires Four Hands to
    Open, Making Powerful Statement About Consent," CBS

News, April 9, 2019, https://www.cbsnews.com/news/consent
-condom-requires-four-hands-to-open-making-powerful
-statement-about-consent/.

5 "The Love Contract," *Chappelle's Show*, Comedy Central,
#ComedyTBT, Facebook, accessed June 20, 2019, https://
www.facebook.com/ComedyCentral/videos/10155999554714
030/?v=10155999554714030.

6 "The Love Contract," *Chappelle's Show*, Comedy Central,
YouTube, accessed June 20, 2019. https://www.youtube.com
/watch?v=ItH2J7T8LSk.

7 "The Blood," *Seinfeld*, NBC, original air date October 16, 1997.

8 https://www.rainn.org/statistics/victims-sexual-violence/, accessed August 3, 2019.

9 Patricia Tjaden and Nancy Thoennes, "Prevalence, Incidence
and Consequences of Violence Against Women Survey," 1998,
National Institute of Justice and Centers for Disease Control
and Prevention, https://www.ncjrs.gov/pdffiles/172837.pdf.

10 Ibid.

11 "Victims of Sexual Violence: Statistics," RAINN, https://www
.rainn.org/statistics/victims-sexual-violence/, accessed August
3, 2019.

12 Katie Heaney, "Almost No One Is Falsely Accused of Rape,"
The Cut.com, October 5, 2018, https://www.thecut.com/article
/false-rape-accusations.html.

13 Jesse David Fox, "Aziz Ansari Reflects on Sexual-Misconduct
Allegation at His NYC Pop-up Show," Vulture.com, February
12, 2019, https://www.vulture.com/2019/02/aziz-ansari-sexual
-misconduct-allegation-new-york-village-underground-show
.html.

Chapter 3: WORK

1 LeanIn.Org and SurveyMonkey survey, February 22–March
1, 2019, https://leanin.org/sexual-harassment-backlash-survey
-results.

2 Justine Harman and Benjy Hanesen-Bundy, "What 1,147 Men

Really Think About #MeToo: A Glamour x GQ Survey," May 30, 2018, https://www.glamour.com/story/men-metoo-survey -glamour-gq.

3 "If You Don't Have Anything Nice to Say, SAY IT IN ALL CAPS," *This American Life*, Public Radio International, January 23, 2015, https://www.thisamericanlife.org/545/transcript.

4 "Employment Law Alliance Survey Takes American Pulse on #MeToo and Workplace Harassment," March 7, 2018, Employment Law Alliance, https://www.ela.law/articles/employment -law-alliance-survey-takes-american-pulse-on-metoo-and -workplace-harassment-.

5 Ellen Carol DuBois and Lynn Dumenil, *Through Women's Eyes: An American History with Documents* (Boston: Bedford/St. Martin's, 2016), 487.

6 Ashley Parker, "Karen Pence Is the Vice President's 'Prayer Warrior,' Gut Check and Shield," *Washington Post*, March 28, 2017, https://www.washingtonpost.com/politics/karen-pence -is-the-vice-presidents-prayer-warrior-gut-check-and-shield /2017/03/28/3d7a26ce-0a01-11e7-8884-96e6a6713f4b_story .html?utm_term=.63ff4abae5d3.

7 Gillian Tan and Katia Porzecanski, "Wall Street Rule for the #MeToo Era: Avoid Women at All Cost," *Bloomberg*, December 3, 2018, https://www.bloomberg.com/news/articles/2018-12 -03/a-wall-street-rule-for-the-metoo-era-avoid-women-at-all -cost.

8 Valentina Zarya, "The Share of Female CEOs in the Fortune 500 Dropped by 25% in 2018," *Fortune*, May 21, 2018, http:// fortune.com/2018/05/21/women-fortune-500-2018/.

9 "The Gender Wage Gap: 2017 Earnings Differences by Gender, Race, and Ethnicity," Institute for Women's Policy Research, September 2018, https://iwpr.org/wp-content/uploads /2018/09/C473.pdf.

10 Alan Jope, "Gender Equality Is 170 Years Away. We Cannot Wait That Long," World Economic Forum, January 19, 2017, https://www.weforum.org/agenda/2017/01/gender-equality -is-170-years-away-we-cannot-wait-that-long/.

11 "Thirty-Eight Percent of Workers Have Dated a Co-Worker, Finds CareerBuilder Survey," CareerBuilder.com, February 12, 2014, https://www.careerbuilder.com/share/aboutus/press releasesdetail.aspx?sd=2%2F13%2F2014&id=pr803&ed=12%2F31%2F2014.

12 "Online Dating Statistics," ReportLinker, February 9, 2017 https://www.reportlinker.com/insight/finding-love-online.html.

13 Billy Graham, *Just as I Am: The Autobiography of Billy Graham* (New York: HarperCollins Worldwide, 1997).

14 Albert Burneko, "What Does Mike Pence Think Happens at Restaurants?" *Deadspin*, March 30, 2017, https://adequateman.deadspin.com/what-does-mike-pence-think-happens-at-restaurants-1793821393.

Chapter 4: MONEY

1 Erin Rehel and Emily Baxter, "Men, Fathers, and Work-Family Balance," Center for American Progress, February 4, 2015 https://www.americanprogress.org/issues/women/reports/2015/02/04/105983/men-fathers-and-work-family-balance/.

2 "The Shriver Report Snapshot: An Insight into the 21st Century Man," A Woman's Nation, 2015, http://www.shrivermedia.com/wp-content/uploads/2016/05/FINAL-Shriver-Report-Snapshot-Press-Release.pdf.

3 N. Gregory Makiw, "Why Aren't More Men Working?" *New York Times*, June 15, 2018, https://www.nytimes.com/2018/06/15/business/men-unemployment-jobs.html.

4 "Percentage of the U.S. population who have completed four years of college or more from 1940 to 2018, by gender," February 2019, https://www.statista.com/statistics/184272/educational-attainment-of-college-diploma-or-higher-by-gender/.

5 "Educational Attainment in the United States: 2017," United States Census Bureau, December 14, 2017, https://www.census.gov/data/tables/2017/demo/education-attainment/cps-detailed-tables.html.

6 Tara Siegel Bernard, "To Buy or Rent a Home? Weighing Which Is Better," *New York Times*, April 1, 2016, https://www.nytimes.com/2016/04/02/your-money/to-buy-or-rent-a-home-weighing-which-is-better.html.

7 "A Look at the Shocking Student Loan Debt Statistics for 2019," Student Loan Hero, February 4, 2019, https://studenthero.com/student-loan-debt-statistics/.

8 Lawrence F. Katz and Alan B. Krueger, "The Rise and Nature of Alternative Work Arrangements in the United States, 1995–2015," Princeton University and NBER, March 29, 2016, https://krueger.princeton.edu/sites/default/files/akrueger/files/katz_krueger_cws_-_march_29_20165.pdf.

9 Elaine Pofeldt, "Obama: Is the Job of the Future a Freelance One?" CNBC, January 29, 2014, https://www.cnbc.com/2014/01/29/obama-is-the-job-of-the-future-a-freelance-one.html.

10 "2018 Better Money Habits Millennial Report," Bank of America, Winter 2018, https://bettermoneyhabits.bankofamerica.com/content/dam/bmh/pdf/ar6vnln9-boa-bmh-millennial-report-winter-2018-final2.pdf.

11 "Sallie Krawcheck on Power, Financial Feminism and Closing the Gender Money Gap," *Hiding in the Bathroom, Forbes*, April 25, 2017, https://www.forbes.com/sites/morraaaronsmele/2017/04/25/sallie-krawcheck-on-power-financial-feminism-and-closing-the-gender-money-gap/#1b1859a16901.

12 "Suze Orman, Author of Women & Money," *So Money with Farnoosh Torabi*, episode 792, October 8, 2018, audio used with permission of *Money* magazine, http://podcast.farnoosh.tv/episode/suze-orman/.

13 Dana Goodyear, "At a Feminist Pop-Up, Cash Is Queen," *New Yorker*, April 23, 2019, https://www.newyorker.com/news/california-chronicles/at-a-feminist-finance-pop-up-cash-is-queen.

14 "Suze Orman, Author of Women & Money."

15 Farnoosh Torabi, *When She Makes More: 10 Rules for Breadwinning Women* (New York: Penguin, 2014).

16 Arlie Hochschild and Anne Machung, *The Second Shift: Working Families and the Revolution at Home*, rev. ed. (New York: Penguin, 2012).

17 Motoko Rich, "Japan's Working Mothers: Record Responsibilities, Little Help from Dads," *New York Times*, February 2, 2019, https://www.nytimes.com/2019/02/02/world/asia/japan-working-mothers.html.

18 U.S. Census Bureau, "Decennial Censuses, 1890 to 1940, and Current Population Survey, Annual Social and Economic Supplements, 1947 to 2018."

19 Charlotte Cowles, "When Two Bank Accounts Become One," The Cut, April 12, 2019 https://www.thecut.com/2019/04/should-you-merge-bank-accounts-in-a-relationship.html.

20 J. Gladstone, E. N. Garbinsky, and C. Mogilner, "Pooling Finances and Relationship Satisfaction" (UCLA working paper, 2018).

21 Ibid.

22 Dr. Jenn Mann, "The One Thing Couples Need to Do to Stop Fighting About Money" *InStyle*, August 22, 2018, https://www.instyle.com/lifestyle/couples-stop-fighting-about-money.

23 Diane Harris, "Poll: How Husbands and Wives Really Feel About Their Finances," Money.com, June 1, 2014, http://money.com/money/2800576/love-money-by-the-numbers/.

Chapter 5: **PARENTING**

1 Yash S. Khandwala, Chiyuan A. Zhang, Ying Lu, and Michael L. Eisenberg, "The Age of Fathers in the USA Is Rising: An Analysis of 168,867,480 births from 1972 to 2015," *Human Reproduction* 32, no. 10 (October 2017): 2110–16, https://doi.org/10.1093/humrep/dex267.

2 Robbie H. Harris, *It's Not the Stork! A Book About Girls, Boys, Babies, Bodies, Families, and Friends* (Cambridge, MA: Candlewick Press, 2008).

3 Tim Kasser, Richard Koestner, and Natasha Lekes, "Early Family Experiences and Adult Values: A 26-Year, Prospective

Longitudinal Study," *Personality and Social Psychology Bulletin* 28, no. 6 (June 2002): 826–35, doi:10.1177/0146167202289011.

4   Darci Walker, "Parenting in a #MeToo World," PDX Parent, January 24, 2018, https://www.pdxparent.com/metoo/?doing _wp_cron=1554120102.1446869373321533203125.

5   David McGlynn, "In the #MeToo Era, Raising Boys to Be Good Guys," *New York Times*, June 1, 2018, https://www.ny times.com/2018/06/01/well/family/metoo-sons-sexual -harassment-parenting-boys.html.

6   P. Glick and S. T. Fiske, "The Ambivalent Sexism Inventory: Differentiating Hostile and Benevolent Sexism," *Journal of Personality and Social Psychology* 70, no. 3 (1996): 491–512, http:// dx.doi.org/10.1037/0022-3514.70.3.491.

7   "It's sad to me that we live in a world where a lot of men refrain from complimenting or being friendly to women because they fear that this will be perceived as sexual harassment," @Steffi _Cole, Twitter, April 5, 2019, https://twitter.com/Steffi_Cole /status/1114347356974125057.

Chapter 6: **FRIENDS**

1   *Access Hollywood* off-screen audiotape, NBC Universal, September 2005.

2   Second Presidential Debate, Washington University in St. Louis, October 9, 2016, debate.wustl.edu.

3   "locker-room" search on Merriam-Webster.com, accessed June 21, 2019, https://www.merriam-webster.com/dictionary /locker-room.

4   Don A. Vaughn, Ricky R. Savjani, Mark S. Cohen, and David M. Eagleman, "Empathic Neural Responses Predict Group Allegiance," *Frontiers in Human Neuroscience* 12 (2018), https:// www.frontiersin.org/article/10.3389/fnhum.2018.00302.

5   R. F. Baumeister and M. R. Leary, "The Need to Belong: Desire for Interpersonal Attachments as a Fundamental Human Motivation," *Psychological Bulletin* 117, no. 3 (1995): 497–529, http://dx.doi.org/10.1037/0033-2909.117.3.497.

6   Elizabeth Levy Paluck, Hana Shepherd, and Peter M. Aro-
now, "Changing Climates of Conflict: A Social Network Ex-
periment in 56 Schools," *Proceedings of the National Academy
of Sciences* 113, no. 3 (January 2016): 566–71, doi:10.1073
/pnas.1514483113.

7   L. E. Williams and J. A. Bargh, "Experiencing Physical Warmth
Promotes Interpersonal Warmth," *Science* 322, no. 5901 (2008):
606–707, doi:10.1126/science.1162548.

8   Vaughn et al., "Empathic Neural Responses Predict Group
Allegiance."

9   *Stand By Me*, Columbia Pictures, 1986.

10 "Suicide Statistics," American Foundation for Suicide Prevention, accessed June 21, 2019, https://afsp.org/about-suicide
/suicide-statistics/.

11 A. J. Kposowa, "Divorce and Suicide Risk," *Journal of Epidemiology & Community Health* 57 (2003): 993.

12 "Survey of People with Lived Experience of Mental Health
Problems Reveals Men Less Likely to Seek Medical Support,"
Mental Health Foundation, November 6, 2016, https://www
.mentalhealth.org.uk/news/survey-people-lived-experience
-mental-health-problems-reveals-men-less-likely-seek-medical.

13 Bridget K. Gorman and Jen'nan Ghazal Read, "Why Men Die
Younger Than Women," *Geriatrics and Aging* 10, no. 3 (2007):
182–91.

14 "A woman's idea of 'Let just be friends' is 'Hey listen to all
my problems and keep me company . . . while I have sex with
someone else,'" Twitter, September 13, 2017, https://twitter
.com/ur_so_cool_nol/status/908185028445786112?lang=en.

Chapter 7: **SELF, HEALTH, AND PORN**

1   E. N. Karakis and R. F. Levant, "Is Normative Male Alexithymia Associated with Relationship Satisfaction, Fear of Intimacy
and Communication Quality Among Men in Relationships?"
Journal of Men's Studies 20, no. 3 (2012): 179–86.

2   Lorna Collier, "Why We Cry: New Research Is Opening Eyes

to the Psychology of Tears," *Monitor on Psychology* 45, no. 2 (February 2014), https://www.apa.org/monitor/2014/02/cry.

3 Ibid.

4 Sherry L. Murphy, Jiaquan Xu, Kenneth D. Kochanek, and Elizabeth Arias, "Mortality in the United States," 2017, NCHS Data Brief, No. 328, November 2018.

5 Holly Hedegaard, Arialdi M. Miniño, and Margaret Warner, "Drug Overdose Deaths in the United States, 1999–2017," NCHS Data Brief, No. 329, November 2018.

6 American Psychological Association, Boys and Men Guidelines Group (2018). APA guidelines for psychological practice with boys and men, retrieved from http://www.apa.org/about/policy/psychological-practice-boys-men-guidelines.pdf.

7 Mark Greene, *The Little #MeToo Book for Men* (New York: ThinPlay Partners, 2018).

8 Eddie Kim, "Why Millennial Men Don't Go to Therapy," *Mel*, accessed June 20, 2019, https://melmagazine.com/en-us/story/why-millennial-men-dont-go-to-therapy.

9 Philip Eil, "Here's Why It's Still Really Hard to Get Men to Go to Therapy," Vice.com, November 22, 2017, https://www.vice.com/en_us/article/43nzag/men-dont-go-therapy-mental-health.

10 *The Jump* interview with Dwyane Wade, ESPN, April 5, 2019, https://www.espn.com/nba/story/_/id/26449116/try-therapy-ease-void-retirement.

11 "Friendos" (Featuring A$AP Rocky), *Saturday Night Live*, NBC, May 5, 2018, https://www.youtube.com/watch?v=7oPe80mdcZg.

12 W.P. Hammond, "Taking It Like a Man: Masculine Role Norms as Moderators of the Racial Discrimination-Depressive Symptoms Association Among African American Men," *American Journal of Public Health*, May 2012, https://www.ncbi.nlm.nih.gov/pubmed/22401515/.

13 Sidney H. Hankerson, Derek Suite, and Rahn K. Bailey, "Treatment Disparities Among African American Men with

Depression: Implications for Clinical Practice," *J Health Care Poor Underserved* 2015, 26(1): 21–34, doi:10.1353/hpu .2015.0012.

14 Keko Nishi, Mental Health Among Asian-Americans, American Psychological Association, 2016, retrieved from http:// www.apa.org/pi/oema/resources/ethnicity-health/asian -american/article-mental-health.aspx.

15 Rachel Nuwer, "What If Women Were Physically Stronger Than Men?" BBC, October 30, 2017. http://www.bbc.com /future/story/20171027-what-if-women-were-physically -stronger-than-men.

16 Ian Janssen, Steven B. Heymsfield, ZiMian Wang, and Robert Ross, "Skeletal Muscle Mass and Distribution in 468 Men and Women Aged 18–88 Yr," *Journal of Applied Physiology*, July 2000, https://doi.org/10.1152/jappl.2000.89.1.81.

17 "2018 Year in Review," PornHub.com, December 11, 2018, https://www.pornhub.com/insights/2018-year-in-review.

Chapter 8: **MEDIA**

1 Joe Coscarelli and Melena Ryzik, "Ryan Adams Dangled Success. Women Say They Paid a Price," *New York Times*, February 13, 2019, https://www.nytimes.com/2019/02/13/arts/music /ryan-adams-women-sex.html.

2 Joe DeRogatis, "Inside the Pied Piper of R&B's 'Cult'" *Buzz-Feed*, July 17, 2017, https://www.buzzfeednews.com/article/jim derogatis/parents-told-police-r-kelly-is-keeping-women-in-a-cult.

3 *Surviving R. Kelly*, Lifetime, A&E Television Networks, January 2019.

4 "Everything is amazing and no one is happy": from Louis C.K. interview on *Late Night with Conan O'Brien*, NBC, Fall 2008.

5 Melena Ryzik, Cara Buckley, and Jodi Kantor, "Louis C.K. Is Accused by 5 Women of Sexual Misconduct," *New York Times*, November 9, 2017, https://www.nytimes.com/2017/11/09 /arts/television/louis-ck-sexual-misconduct.html.

6 Matt Damon interview with *Popcorn with Peter Travers*, ABC News, December 14, 2017, https://abcnews.go.com/Entertain ment/matt-damon-opens-harvey-weinstein-sexual-harassment -confidentiality/story?id=51792548.

7 "God God, SERIOUSLY?" Twitter, December 15, 2017, https: //twitter.com/driverminnie/status/941733516999405568.

8 *Today* show interview with Matt Damon and Kathie Lee Gifford, NBC, January, 16, 2018.

9 *The Age of Spin: Dave Chappelle Live at the Hollywood Palladium*, premiered March 21, 2017, Netflix.

10 Louis C.K., "Louis C.K. Responses to Accusations: These Stories Are True," November 10, 2017, https://www.nytimes .com/2017/11/10/arts/television/louis-ck-statement.html.

11 Mary Elizabeth Williams, "Louis C.K. Is Back, and It's Bad," *Salon*, December 31, 2018, https://www.salon.com/2018/12/31 /louis-c-k-is-back-and-its-bad-leaked-stand-up-set-shows -hes-lost-more-than-his-reputation/.

12 "Our Own Thoughts vs. Media Influence," Penn State, October 26, 2014, https://sites.psu.edu/aspsy/2014/10/26/our-own -thoughts-vs-media-influence/.

13 S. Stack, "Media Coverage as a Risk Factor in Suicide," *Journal of Epidemiology & Community Health* 57 (2003): 238–40.

Conclusion: **WHERE DO WE GO FROM HERE?**

1 "Consent," Vice News, September 29, 2018, https://www.you tube.com/watch?v=DhFyGz8wQaY.

2 Ibid.

3 "Don't Let Him Wipe or Flush," *Harmontown*, January 10, 2018, https://www.harmontown.com/2018/01/episode-dont -let-him-wipe-or-flush/.

4 "Get a Spine!" *This American Life*, Public Radio International, May 10, 2019, https://www.thisamericanlife.org/674/transcript.

5 Ibid.

6 "What Is Restorative Justice," RestorativeJustice.org, accessed June 21, 2019, http://restorativejustice.org/restorative-justice

/about-restorative-justice/tutorial-intro-to-restorative-justice /lesson-1-what-is-restorative-justice/#sthash.RdHl4hc8.dpbs.

7 Jill S. Levenson and Alissa Ackerman, "The Stanford Rape Case: Maybe We're Having the Wrong Conversation?" *Psychology Today*, July 19, 2016, https://www.psychologytoday.com/intl /blog/the-guest-room/201607/the-stanford-rape-case?amp.

8 Rabbi Danya Ruttenberg, "Famous Abusers Seek Easy Forgiveness. Rosh Hashanah Teaches Us Repentance Is Hard," *Washington Post*, September 6, 2018, https://www.washington post.com/outlook/famous-abusers-seek-easy-forgiveness -rosh-hashanah-teaches-us-repentance-is-hard/2018/09/06 /c2dc2cac-b0ab-11e8-9a6a-565d92a3585d_story.html?no redirect=on&utm_term=.d15683a5696b.

9 Brené Brown, *The Call to Courage*, Netflix, May 2019.